TAPAS

Classic small dishes from Spain

Elisabeth Luard

This paperback edition published in 2017 by
Grub Street
4 Rainham Close
London
SW11 6SS

Email: food@grubstreet.co.uk
Web: www.grubstreet.co.uk
Twitter: @grub_street
Facebook: Grub Street Publishing

Text © Elisabeth Luard 2017
Copyright this edition © Grub Street 2017
Photography by Michelle Garrett
Food styling by Jayne Cross
First published by Martin Books as *The La Ina Book of Tapas* in 1989

A CIP catalogue record for this book is available from
the British Library.

ISBN 978-1-910690-34-5

Printed and bound in India

CONTENTS

RECIPE NOTES

All recipes give ingredients in metric, imperial and cup measures. Use any one set of measurements, but not a mixture, in any one recipe.

All spoon measures are given in level spoons, unless otherwise stated.

1 tablespoon = one 15 ml spoon; 1 teaspoon = one 5 ml spoon.

Eggs are standard (size 2-3), unless otherwise stated.

Two mouthfuls make up a tapa portion, served on a small oval plate or saucer. More expensive dishes, or larger servings, can be ordered as a whole 'ration'. This is a plateful: a small dinner plate crammed to capacity. Half-a-ration is a side-plate full. Quantity is dictated by plate-size. A small amount of food is never served in the middle of a large plate, as the aim is to appear generous and hospitable.

Breadcrumbs are white. Spaniards do not really approve of brown bread, although attitudes are changing in line with the rest of Europe. Make your own with stale bread, sliced and dried in a very low oven until it is crisp and pale gold. Crush in a food processor, or wrap the crisped bread in a clean towel and run a rolling pin over it until it is thoroughly crumbled. Store in an airtight tin and use as required.

The traditional Spanish sherry glass is the copita. It is tall, thin and tulip-shaped. Never fill it more than two-thirds full to appreciate the delicate aroma of the wine.

A small glass is a sherry glass filled to within a thumb-width of the top. A wine glass is about 125ml.

A finger's width/depth is 1.5 cm. 2 fingers width/depth is 3 cm.

Sherry vinegar is a by-product of the sherry industry. It is a fine, oak-flavoured, strong vinegar which adds richness and distinction to a dish. It must be used sparingly and diluted with water if the recipe calls for a large volume of liquid. To make vinaigrette with sherry vinegar, use a 1:6 proportion vinegar to oil instead of the usual 1:4. Substitute wine or cider vinegar, if unavailable (balsamic is too sweet).

Dry-leaf herbs – thyme, rosemary, sage, oregano – weigh just about the same dried or fresh: one can be substituted for the other. Parsley, marjoram and mint must always be used fresh.

INTRODUCTION

Tapas, as I'm sure you already know, are those delicious little titbits served as the accompaniment to a glass of wine. You'll find them in their original form in the bars of Seville in Andalucía, where the native wine is the clean, straw-pale nectar of Jerez. Until very recently, the price of the glass always included a tiny dish of the house speciality. Nowadays it is more likely that the tapas will be priced and served in full or half portions – on one plate, but with a fork for each participant. But the tapa itself, a 'lid' for the glass it accompanies, is traditionally no more than a mouthful.

'Que hay para tapar?' 'What is there to pick at?' is the question every bartender expects to hear as he takes the order for a glass of wine. He'll answer with a litany, rhythmic, almost singing. He can repeat it, too, if asked – word for word, rhyme for rhyme.

Tapas embody a way of life. Southern Spain lives outdoors, and in the long light summers, day and night merge into each other. Mediterranean sunshine, golden beaches, fertile valleys, white-washed villages and herb-scented hillsides, mark what to those of us who live under chilly northern skies as the road to happiness.

The Spaniard, as with all Mediterranean natives, is naturally garrulous. The world and his wife loves company, sits out on the street of an evening or takes a gentle saunter round the village square, exchanging news, inspecting each others' impeccably turned-out infants and indulging, where appropriate, in a little light flirtation. The tapa habit is a reflection of this natural companionability, allowing the freedom to wander, lean an elbow on the bar, chat to acquaintances, settle down at a table under the awning and keep an eye on the children. And the tiny dishes of food which accompany the wine keep the wanderer comparatively sober and amiable. As Don Quixote was to the novel – picaresque, progressing in short bursts of self-contained drama – so tapas are to a conventional meal.

The *romerías* – local religious pilgrimages which turn into all-day picnics – reflect a national delight in getting out and about on high days and holidays, and the rituals of the tapa bar seems to be an everyday extension of this pleasure. The habit is essentially peripatetic, a wander from bar to bar – in search of not only special dishes, but also entertainment. While the television rumbles on in one corner, an electronic Ancient Mariner who performs much the same function and to whom no one is obliged to listen, the life of the neighbourhood is reflected in the comings and goings outside and within.

It was not until I went to live in the 1960's with my novelist husband and our four young children in a remote Andalucían valley that I learnt to appreciate the pleasures of this thoroughly Spanish way of eating. Long before the fashion for open kitchens in Michelin-starred restaurants, the humble provider of tapas cooked to order and set everything out on display. His clientele wouldn't have it any other way, perhaps because the nation is visually articulate – think Goya, Velazquez, Picasso – and likes to know what it's getting.

Our house was buried in a cork-oak forest high in the hills overlooking the southernmost point of Europe, halfway between Algeciras, a busy seaport, and Tarifa, a small fortified harbour town, once a Phoenician stronghold. The region itself, Andalucía, had been under Moorish rule for seven centuries, and their culinary influence remained in the use of spicing, a taste for almond-based sweetmeats and a light hand with frying pan. It was the Muslim presence at both ends of the Mediterranean – the Ottoman Empire on the east and the caliphs of Al-Andaluz in the west – which ensured that iron replaced earthenware as the cooking-implement of choice.

Meanwhile, once the children were settled in local schools, we began to look around for local entertainment. At the time there were no theatres nearer than Malaga. The red light district of Algeciras was the only area where good flamenco could be found – and that was not really family viewing. Films were poorly dubbed, cinema accommodation primitive and television in its squalling infancy. Feria – Spain's local carnival – brought circus and bullfights and dancing to Algeciras in June, in September to Tarifa. For the rest of the year, we instituted a regular Saturday evening family tapa-hunt. With four children under ten we were perfectly in tune with local habit. In public places in Spain, children tumble underfoot everywhere. Babies and children accompany their parents on their evening outings, slumbering on a maternal shoulder when they're tired, or curling up on in a corner while the adults gossip and flirt and argue over their heads.

From an early age children are given a splash of wine in their water – usually carbonated sweetened water known as *gaseosa* – to qualify them for a little tapa along with the grownups. The atmosphere is leisurely – browsing and grazing are not exactly urgent occupations – and conversation is the only necessary accompaniment to a tapa. That and the pale dry wines of Jerez or Sanlucar or Puerto de Santa Maria, the only wines made by the solera method, distinctive in flavour and fragrance. Or even the good red wine of Rioja or Valdepeñas or Jumilla if that's what pleases you best. But there's no doubt that the dry pale sherries of Jerez go wonderfully well with certain dishes. Particularly those, when, as they say in Cadiz, the very sea-spray has been dipped in batter and fried in the olive oil of Sevilla. Or Toledo. Or Ronda. Or wherever you feel the rich green juice of the Mediterranean's oldest cultivated fruit is at its best.

Since we did not live in a village, we would make our way to our chosen locale and do the rounds. The nearest settlement, Pelayo, was famous for its bakery, and the roadside bar served big chunks of bread with tiny bowls of snails in paprika sauce. The secondary bar, tucked away behind, was always full of old men playing draughts – and the kitchen had wonderful wild rabbit cooked with garlic. So that made a fine enough evening. If we turned east down the road towards the Atlantic we could have spider-crabs and seasnails in a bar set into the Moorish battlements of Tarifa, and then go on further, to the chozo down by the beach at Punta Paloma, for deep-fried quail and the fattest crispest chips in Spain.

Algeciras, on the Mediterranean side, offered the more sophisticated delicacies of a busy seaport. Down by the harbour was a bar which served big pink prawns as firm as lobster, baby cuttlefish fried to perfection, clams and razor shells opened briefly on a scalding hotplate and served with quartered lemons. And in the deserted market place someone would have set up a brazier to blister juicy octopus tentacles over the hot coals. Unlike most of the locals, we usually found we could not manage to tuck into a large meal afterwards – a shortcoming which had something to do with our English habit of still taking tea and this-and-that throughout the day.

In a simple bar in a small village, the tapa offered with your glass of wine will be correspondingly modest. A few home-cured green olives, a bit of local goat's cheese, a cube of Spanish tortilla – the thick potato omelette any Spanish housewife seems to be able to turn out to perfection. Big cities and towns – Barcelona, Seville, Malaga, Granada, Madrid – reflect in their bars and restaurants the affluence of their citizens. Customers progress from venue to venue, proud of their knowledge of house specialities – like truffle hounds scenting out the treasure.

Raw materials are very important in the cooking of Spain, as with all uncomplicated cuisines. Good bread and chorizo, the freshest of shellfish, a way of leaching and flavouring the best and plumpest of olives – each bar, chozo and tasca will have its own specialities. These may simply be the best salt-dried mountain ham – maybe a pata negra, black-foot ham from Jabugo; or a well-matured cheese – a fine Manchego or a leaf-wrapped Cabrales. Or the house fame might rest on a little scalding casserole of angulas – baby eels bathed in olive oil and spiked with chilli. Or even some small delicacy which reflects the skill of the cook with the frying pan. No one fries better than a Spaniard – and among Spaniards, none better than the Andaluz.

Kitchen equipment dictates as firmly as ingredients. The plancha – a flat metal griddle heated with a gas jet or charcoal underneath – is used to grill sardines, prawns, thin slices of tuna or swordfish, pork fillet marinated with garlic and paprika. In Seville I have seen a heavy old smoothing iron smacked on top of a chop to speed up the cooking process. In the hills behind Cordoba there is a bar which serves only quails eggs fried on the plancha and dishes them on a piece of bread cut to scale. But the most basic cooking-tool, a long metal tin filled with white-hot charcoal, dates back to the days of the Moors and is set up in the street in feria-time by fez-hatted travelling peddlars who grill Moorish-spiced kebabs, *pinchitos* – the name translates as 'little thorns' – to order for an eager queue of customers.

Which is not to overlook Spain's original frying-pan, the *cazuela*, a shallow earthenware casserole of variable diameter glazed on the inside but not on the outside and which serves for both cooking and serving. A cazuela needs to be tempered before it can be placed on a naked flame and all housewives have their own method of making a new cazuela fireproof: the most popular method is to rub the glazed surface with a cut clove of garlic, fill the dish to the brim with cold water and set it in a hot oven till the water boils dry. Once tempered, the cazuela holds its heat for at least 10 minutes, allowing the contents to continue to cook. You'll find single-portion cazuelas used to present luxurious little tapas such as *gambas pilpil* (peeled prawns bubbled up in hot oil with garlic and chilli), *angulas al ajillo* (pin-sized baby eels cooked in the same way); and, on the Basque seaboard, hake-throats, *kokochas*, which produce their own creamy sauce when shaken in the cazuela over a high heat with oil and garlic. The same cazuela is used to fry eggs with ham or scramble them with wild mushrooms or the short spears of asparagus-sprue gathered in spring, or simply to reheat a ladleful of something from the pot simmering on the back of the stove.

Tapas can be as simple as a saucer of anchovy-stuffed olives and a sliver of salty cheese, or a little taste of a slow-cooked herb-scented stew, or a mouthful of something so exotic you might not come by it in any other way. The only rule is that a tapa is something to be savoured at leisure and in good company, with a chilled glass of one of the straw-pale wines of Jerez or the red wine of Rioja or any of the other wines made with such skill throughout the peninsula.

With this in mind, I hope the recipes in this book will encourage you to get the tapa habit. Then, secure in the certainty that all's well with the world, we may raise our glasses together in the traditional Spanish toast, '!Salud, amor y pesetas!'– 'Here's to health, love and wealth!' – to which the reply, 'y tiempo para gustarlos' guarantees the only thing most of us lack, time enough for enjoyment.

BASICS

Although tapas only officially appeared during the last century – they were first recorded in Seville – the tradition is part of a far older one: that of hospitality and the desire to honour a guest.

The question '?quiere algo para picar?' – 'would you like something to nibble?' – always accompanies the offer of a glass of sherry in a Spanish household or bar. It is a matter of pride. Tapas are essentially small bits and pieces: quantity defines them, with quality dependent on the most freely-available local raw materials.

If there are snails at the bottom of your garden, snails is the tapa you will offer your guests. If the fishermen have returned with more sardines than they can sell, the local bar will serve grilled (broiled) sardines as the tapa. If the housewife made a good chick-pea stew yesterday, an honoured guest will be served a little saucer of that.

As well as these small opportunist snacks, there is a repertoire of everyday tapas, usually based on larder stores, which can range from a handful of salty biscuits to a dish of home-cured olives, from a plate of salt-cured ham cut from the family's Christmas treat, to a bit of good fresh country bread with savoury dripping.

Pickled olives
Aceitunas aliñadas

Spain exports large quantities of table olives, specialising in ma-

chine-pitted green olives stuffed with strips of pimento, whole almonds, tiny onions, or anchovies. Home-cured olives, *aceitunas aliñadas*, are the ones most frequently encountered in the tapa bars of the south.

Olives are a seasonal crop, gathered in the autumn in Andalucía when they are sold fresh, varying in size from fruit as large as a quail's egg to fruit smaller than a hazelnut, and varying in colour from bright green to pale mauve, depending on the degree of ripeness. In Spain, olives for pickling are harvested before they have a chance to ripen to black – the stage at which they are pressed for oil. The fresh fruits are cracked and soaked in pure water, or, if they are to be left whole, in water with lye (a leached solution), until they lose their bitterness. Then they are put in an earthenware crock with a loose wooden lid, to pickle submerged in a strong aromatic brine. Flavourings include herbs, garlic and wine vinegar, with sometimes a chilli or two, and maybe chunks of lemon or bitter orange to add flavour and piquancy. As the year wears on, the olives become sweeter and more pickled as they ferment, a natural process as with wine – by which time the next year's crop will be ready.

Those who do not pickle their own can select from a dozen or so different sizes and marinades on display in big plastic buckets in the market place. A passable imitation of home-cured olives can be made by marinating commercially-prepared olives for a week or two in a home-made brine. I used to pickle my own fresh olives every year in more or less the same mix: use the recipe as a guideline – add dried chillis for a little heat, thyme instead of fennel.

makes 10 tapa portions

500 g/1 lb can or jar of whole unpitted green olives
4 whole garlic cloves
1 lemon or bitter orange
1-2 sprigs of thyme
1 tablespoon coriander seeds
1 dried fennel stick, broken into short lengths
1 small glass of sherry or wine vinegar

Drain the olives and bash them lightly with a rolling pin. Carefully burn the garlic in a naked flame until the papery cover blackens, then crush a little. Cut a slice from the middle of the lemon or orange and reserve, then chunk the rest.

Pack the olives, garlic and chunked lemon or orange in a screw-top jar, sprinkling in the aromatics as you go, then add the vinegar and enough water to cover. Top with the lemon or orange slice to keep the olives submerged. You should not need extra salt – the conserved olives are usually salty enough.

Lid tightly and keep in the fridge for at least a week. Bring them up to room temperature before serving.

Spiced peanuts
Cacahuetes con sal picante

Salted nuts are a popular luxury on the tapa table, though these days almonds are often replaced by the cheaper imported peanut. Smoked pimentón, if you can get it, will deepen the flavour.

makes 4 tapa portions
250 g/8 oz/1⅓ cups shelled peanuts (unskinned)
1 tablespoon oil
1 teaspoon mild pimentón
1 teaspoon hot pimentón (or powdered chilli)
1 teaspoon ground cumin
1 teaspoon ground coriander
1 teaspoon sea salt

Preheat the oven to Gas Mark 2/150°C/300°F.

Roast the peanuts for 60-75 minutes in the oven. They take longer to roast than most nuts – the result should be golden rather than brown. Toss the roasted nuts with the oil and seasonings and return them to the oven for another 10 minutes, allowing the nuts to absorb the oil and the heat to develop the spices.

Serve them warm.

Salted almonds
Almendras con sal

The Moors planted Spain's almond groves with stock from the Jordan valley – they found the fertile plain of Granada ideal for the cultivation of their favourite nut tree. Almonds are used extensively in Spanish cooking, both whole and ground, in sweetmeats and to thicken sauces. Every feria has its almond-salesman, every spice-merchant his store of almonds. There is nothing like the scent of freshly roasted almonds – for that alone, it's well worth preparing them yourself. They make a lovely squeak as you bite into them. Liberally dusted with salt, they give a fine thirst for the accompanying drink.

makes 4 tapa portions
250 g/8 oz/1⅓ cups almonds (in their skins or blanched)
a little oil (optional)
1 small egg white, forked to blend
1-2 tablespoons fine sea salt

Preheat the oven to Gas Mark 2/150°C/300°F.

Spread the almonds in a roasting tray and toss them with the oil. Roast them in the oven for 40-50 minutes until deliciously golden brown.

Alternatively, dry-fry the almonds gently in a heavy frying pan or skillet until they take a fine roasted colour.

When they are done and piping hot, turn them in the egg white – they will turn glossy – and toss them immediately in the salt. The salt will stick to the almonds, giving them a salty jacket which dries in their heat.

Serve them fresh and warm.

Toasted hazelnuts
Nueces tostadas

Hazelnuts are a wild crop in northern Spain. They are sometimes crushed and used in Catalan cooking to thicken sauces – instead of, or included with, ground almonds. They are served as tapas either plain roasted or roasted and salted. I like the simple rich flavour of the unsalted ones.

makes 4 tapa portions
250g/8 oz/1⅓ cups whole hazelnuts (skinned or unskinned)

Preheat the oven to Gas Mark 2/150°C/300°F.

Toast the hazelnuts in the oven for 50-60 minutes, till the meat turns a pale gold. Serve them warm. A dish of olives (page 12) and a plate of salty crisps (page 29) will complete a simple arrangement of tapas.

Cheese
Queso

Spain boasts a large range of cheeses, from the simplest of fresh curds to sophisticated matured blue-veined cheeses which can give Stilton and Roquefort a run for their money. Although there are many excellent local cheeses, only six have currently been granted Spain's official 'Denomination of Origin' which guarantees their quality. Any of these, served with bread and olives, make a delicious tapa. Manchego is the most widely available outside Spain.

Manchego, Spain's best-known cheese, is a mature hard ewe's milk cheese made on the high plateau of La Mancha in central Spain. It undergoes at least sixty days maturing, and the more expensive 'old' cheeses are left for considerably longer. The cylindrical cheeses weigh between four and eight kilos; they have a pale yellow rind flowered with a greenish-black mould when mature, and a

characteristic plaited pattern round the sides. A whole cheese can be submerged in olive oil for further maturing, when it becomes exquisitely buttery and pungent: there is a tapa bar in Seville which specialises in such oil-matured cheeses, serving them sliced on bread, a background for the oily juices. To serve as a tapa, manchego should be cut in thin slices and arranged in a single layer on a plate, much like serrano ham.

Mahon, a cow's milk cheese from Menorca, can be eaten fresh or matured. Its preparation calls for draining in a linen cloth, a process which gives it its characteristic fold-mark on the upper surface as well as its square form with rounded edges. A whole cheese weighs between one and four kilos. Mahon cheese is served, in its home territory, cut in thin slices, dressed with olive oil and sprinkled with fresh or dried tarragon and pepper.

Idiazábal is, as its name suggests, a speciality of the Basque country. Made exclusively from ewe's milk, it is a whole cheese, cylindrical in shape with a golden rind and a compact pale ivory curd. Each cheese weighs between half and three-and-a-half kilos and is sometimes smoked over beech and hawthorn wood, giving the rind a dark brown colour and the crumb a smoky, nutty flavour. Serve it cut into thin slivers, with bread.

Roncal is a pungent ewe's milk cheese made in the Roncal valley of Navarra – a high mountainous region whose sturdy independent inhabitants played a major part in Aragon's resistance to the Moors. A cylindrical cheese with a hard, straw-coloured rind and firm, slightly aerated texture, it is matured for at least four months. Roncal is only manufactured between December and July. Serve it cut into thin slivers, with bread and perhaps a finely-sliced mild onion.

Cantabria is made exclusively with milk from Friesan cows in the Autonomous Community of Cantabria, where the climate is damp and the meadows are fertile enough to support the herds. The cheese is disc-shaped, with a soft bone-coloured rind and solid creamy texture. It is only lightly matured – for a minimum of seven days. Serve it cut into thin slices, with a few pickled gherkins as the accompaniment.

Cabrales comes from the high mountain valleys on the Asturian side of the Picos de Europa. Like its close cousin Picon – a cheese from the other side of the Picos – this is piquant blue cheese made with a mixture of whole cow's milk and small proportions of goat's and/or ewe's milk. Traditionally it's ripened in curing-caves carved out of the chalky mountainside, like those of Roquefort, for at least two months and came to market, in the old days, wrapped in the dried leaves of maple or plane trees. Locals sometimes mix the cheese with cider to make a powerful potted-cheese spread. To serve as a simple tapa, cut into small cubes and provide cocktail sticks for ease of handling.

Casero or 'household' cheese is a relatively new designation for the traditional semi-matured and matured goats' milk cheeses of Andalucía. If the intention was to store the cheeses from one year to the next, the cheeses were rubbed with olive oil and pimentón, a method which allowed traditionally-prepared home-made cheeses protection from insect-life when stored, as was usual in the old days, on a beam in a current of air. The treatment delivered a depth of flavour which commanded a premium in the marketplace. The texture is crumbly rather than elastic, with a pleasant sharpness and a purity of flavour which works well with fresh or dried figs or quince paste, membrillo.

Salt-cured ham
Jamón serrano

Jamón serrano, 'mountain ham', is the most valued of flavouring ingredients in Spanish cookery. In many kitchens, a whole haunch complete with trotter is often to be seen hanging alongside the obligatory string of dried red sweet peppers and the plait of garlic – although in poorer households this might only be at Christmas. There is always a stall in the market which deals in salted pig products, with a use for every little bit of the precious beast. The best cuts of ham are sliced off very finely to be served just as they are. The well-flavoured chewy little bits from near the bone are used to flavour soups, sauces and croquettes, or they might be fried with eggs, or go to flavour a tortilla; while the bones are sawn up to add richness, along with a piece of creamy yellow ham fat, to a bean stew.

A few rural households still keep a pig or two every year, to eat up the scraps and forage for acorns, roots and berries on the surrounding mountain slopes. I used to keep one for my own family when we lived in Andalucía. Slaughter is usually in the autumn, and if the pig-owner lives in a damp area by the sea, the hams will be sent up to a cousin or friend who lives in the mountains, to be cured in the cold dry air. From this custom has developed a commercial ham-curing industry, with certain mountain villages achieving particular fame for their product.

Jabugo in Huelva, Trevelez in Granada, Montanchez in Caceres, Sotoserrano and Candelario in the province of Salamanca are all well-known for their fine hams. Spain's Ministry of Agriculture has currently granted 'Denomination of Origin' status to the hams of the province of Teruel, and to those of Guijuelo, south east of Salamanca.

The ancient Iberian breed of near-wild pig, the Iberico or pata-negra – black foot for the colour of the trotter – is the original ham-pig of the peninsula and the meat, once cured, was known as serrano or mountain ham, a product in which flavour and density is more important than tenderness. The 1970's saw the introduction of domesticated breeds of pig, larger and more amenable to corralling. These days, the hams of the lean, grey-skinned hump-backed Iberian pig – a distinctive breed with black or reddish bristles – which has been allowed to fatten on acorns and chestnuts in the wild goes to make the prized pata negra. The cheaper hams are made with the meat of the larger imported beasts – Landrace, Duroc, Large White – some of which have recently been successfully cross-bred with the native pigs.

Spanish serrano, as pata negra, is salt-cured and wind-dried without the application of heat or smoke: its closest equivalent is Italian prosciutto. The initial dry-curing of the hams in salt lasts about ten days. After that they are hung up for the winter months in the rafters of an airy attic to cure in the cold dry winds of the sierras. When the weather turns warmer, the hams start to bead with buttery juices, and they are moved to a cool cellar to finish developing their char-

acteristic flavour and texture. Free-range Iberian hams take longer to cure than those from corralled pigs, and are consequently much more expensive. They have very little exterior fat, a beautiful rich marbling of creamy fat throughout the meat, a wonderful deep red-wine colour and an incomparable wild-game flavour.

makes 16 tapa mouthfuls /
allow 50-75 g (2-3 oz) per person as a starter
250 g/8 oz jamón serrano
8 slices of country bread

Wind-cured ham should be very finely sliced – almost transparent. Use a razor-sharp, long, slender, flexible blade such as those used for smoked salmon. The more freshly-sliced, the better it will be. Protect the cut surface of a ham, once started, with strips of its own fat (or greased tinfoil) so that it does not dry out. Serve with bite-sized pieces of bread – either separate or with the ham laid on as a topping.

Paprika sausage
Chorizo

At a rural pig-killing those meaty bits of the household pig which do not go for ham or bacon (tocino) are minced (ground) to make this garlic and paprika-spiced, all-meat sausage. Wind-dried and (sometimes, but not always) lightly smoked, chorizo is often pre-pared commercially in tandem with jamón serrano. These sausages are still made, along with black puddings, by rural housewives as part of their provision for winter. The rinsing and scrubbing of in-testines for stuffing is one of the more leisurely activities of a country *matanza* (pig-killing) – ingenious cooks, in my time some thirty years ago, used a hose-pipe instead of relying on the current of the stream to rinse out the insides of the long tubes.

The housewife makes her chorizo with roughly-chopped lean and fat pork. The meat is seasoned with salt, pepper, paprika, cumin, dried coriander, garlic and red wine, with maybe a bit of chilli or oregano. The mixture is stuffed into sausage casings, and then hung up to dry and cure with, perhaps, the addition of a little light smoking. When making a Spanish stew, these seasonings, plus a length of all-meat pork sausage, will help to reproduce the flavour of Spanish chorizo.

Chorizo can be finished as single lengths, long loops, or knotted into short links of about 25-50g (1-2 oz) a piece. When the chorizo is well-cured (firm and dark) it is often sliced and eaten raw, like Italian salami. The softer, less-cured sausages can be grilled (broiled) whole or sliced and fried as a deliciously piquant tapa. Well-cured tiny ones are delicious flamed in a little warmed brandy, which just singes the skin.

Other such speciality sausages include regional delicacies such as the rosemary-flavoured longaniza, and the Catalan butifarra and Valencian blanquets which replace the chorizo's paprika with cinnamon and nutmeg.

makes 10-12 tapa mouthfuls / serves 2-4 as a starter

**250 g/8 oz finely sliced mature chorizo sausage,
or 375 g/12 oz fresh chorizo, sliced thickly or twisted
into single-mouthful lengths
10-12 small rounds of bread
oil or lard (shortening) for frying (optional)**

If using the mature chorizo, cut the bread slices into quarters. Serve with the sliced raw chorizo.

If the chorizo is fresh, fry it in a drop of olive oil or lard (shortening) – it will soon yield its own fat – until brown and crisp outside but still juicy within. Serve either speared on to bread with cocktail sticks, or with bread fast-fried (but not saturated) in the fat which runs from the chorizo.

Black pudding
Morcilla

Rural Spanish housewives who still keep their own pigs, make their own black puddings with fresh pig's blood at the annual *matanza*. There was a time when all Europe's countrywomen made their own blood-sausages – each to her own regional recipe, including various seasonings, and sometimes barley or oats, rice or breadcrumbs, or whatever suited the climate and local habit.

Spain likes its blood-puddings flavoured with paprika, onions, garlic, cloves, pepper, marjoram, coriander and cumin. My neighbours in Andalucía included small cubes of lean pork and back-fat in their favourite mix – and in some districts rice is added as well. Simmering the loops of black-pudding in a cauldron over a wood-fire in the yard was the last chore of the *matanza*: when I asked my local mentor María how to tell when they were done, she told me they would sing when they were ready. Indeed they did, whistling air through the expanded tiny holes in the casing of intestine.

makes 12-15 tapa mouthfuls / serves 4 as a light meal
(with eggs fried in the morcilla fat)

250 g/8 oz Spanish morcilla, sliced thickly
or 250 g/8 oz black pudding
1-2 tablespoons olive oil or lard (shortening)
1 onion slice, chopped finely
1 garlic clove, crushed
1 teaspoon marjoram
1 teaspoon pimentón
1 teaspoon ground cumin
½ teaspoon ground cloves
½ teaspoon ground coriander
½ teaspoon pepper

to serve
12-15 bite-sized rounds of bread

If your choice is morcilla, fry or grill (broil) it in its own rich aromatic fat. If using the black pudding, cut it into bite-sized pieces. Heat the oil or lard (shortening) in a frying pan (skillet). Fry the onion and garlic gently until soft and pale gold. Add the herbs and spices and the black pudding pieces. Fry the pieces until they are lightly crisp.

Serve hot, speared on to chunks of bread.

Pork drippings
Manteca de cerdo

There are three different flavours of pork dripping: white (sometimes perfumed with garlic and herbs); red (*colorada*) which is flavoured and coloured with pimentón, and a pimentón-coloured dripping in which small pieces of lean pork are preserved (a preparation rather like the French *rilletes*). These flavoured drippings can be bought at the pork-products stall in the market. They are popular as a labourer's breakfast, and any of the three drippings make good simple tapas when spread on bread. Here is an all-purpose pimentón dripping with a little meat for texture and flavour. Save the pork-skin to fry in shallow oil to make crisp, puffed-up pork-scratchings, *chicharros*.

makes 8-10 tapa portions
250 g/8 oz unsalted pork back-fat, cubed small
250 g/8 oz belly pork, cubed small
2 tablespoons paprika
1 teaspoon dried thyme
1 teaspoon dried oregano
2-3 garlic cloves, singed and peeled
1 teaspoon salt

Preheat the oven to Gas Mark 1/140°C/275°F.

Put all the pork fat and belly in a large roasting tin and leave them in the oven for 5-6 hours, until the fat is all rendered. Stir in the spices, herbs and garlic and put it back in the oven to infuse for another hour.

Cool and store. Use as a spread on fresh or toasted bread.

Pork scratchings
Chicharros

These delicious little crisp-fried cracklings are strained out after the pork fat is rendered to make *manteca*. They are the traditional children's treat at the annual pig-killing – the *matanza* – which was not so long ago an important ritual in rural Spanish life.

makes 6 tapa portions
125 g/4 oz/½ cup pure pork lard (shortening)
250 g/8 oz pork skin, sliced into matchsticks
salt

Melt the lard (shortening) in a wide frying pan (skillet). When it is lightly hazed with blue, drop in the matchsticks of pork skin. They will puff up and brown crisp. Drain and sprinkle with salt. They keep well in an airtight tin.

Fresh sausages
Salchichas frescas

Spain's fresh sausages are small, spicy and made of pure pork. They can be a little fatty, so I prefer them fried or grilled (broiled) really crisp. Buy Toulouse sausages, or any all-meat sausage which has no rusk or breadcrumbs to bulk it out. Nutmeg is a popular sausage spicing in Spain, and all recipes include plenty of pepper and usually a little saltpetre to turn them bacon-pink.

makes 20-25 tapa mouthfuls / serves 4 as a starter
500 g/1 lb all-meat pork sausages
1 tablespoon olive oil or lard (shortening)
1 garlic clove, crushed (optional)
½ teaspoon grated nutmeg
fresh tomato sauce (page 176), to serve

Twist the sausages into bite-sized lengths – that is, as long as a joint of your thumb. Fry them in the oil or lard (shortening) until crisp and well-browned, with the garlic, if they were not garlicked already. Sprinkle with the nutmeg.

Serve piping hot, with fresh tomato sauce.

Potato crisps
Patatas fritas

These can be bought hot from the fryer on many a street corner, being a spin-off from Spain's favourite breakfast, churros (long thin doughnut-like fritters). All morning long the frying-kiosks are kept busy supplying everyone from grannies to schoolchildren to businessmen with their morning ration of churros, to be enjoyed in a nearby café with hot milky coffee or chocolate. In the evening the kiosk-cooks use the same equipment to fry crisps, which are also taken to the local café, this time to be enjoyed with a glass of wine.

makes 6 tapa portions
1 kg/2 lb old potatoes
oil for deep-frying (olive with sunflower is perfect)
salt

Wash the potatoes well, dry them thoroughly, and cut them into near-transparent slices (you can peel them if you wish).

Heat the oil until it is hazed with blue. Deep-fry the slices, a handful at a time so that the oil temperature does not drop.

Drain on kitchen paper and sprinkle with salt.
You won't regret the trouble of making your own.

Hot bread with olive oil and garlic
Pan con aceite y ajo

Spanish country bread is excellent, and many Andalucían villages still boast a village baker to supply the most important staple of the rural diet. Close textured and always creamy-white, with a crisp golden-brown crust, country bread is usually sour-dough, with each batch raised with a starter from the day before. This, plus the precise mix and grind of the flour used, and still in some cases the wood used to heat the oven, gives an individual flavour to the product of different bakers. Such bread is sold by weight – value for money is of the essence. The comparative merits of say, the bread of Facinas and the bread of Pelayo, were a keen subject for discussion in my local bar.

Bread with garlic and oil is a favourite Andaluz breakfast, and provides the simplest of tapas – perfect basic materials are all that is required.

makes about 8-10 slices

**500 g/1 lb close-textured country bread (homemade is best)
1 garlic clove, cut in half
4-5 tablespoons extra virgin olive oil**

Warm the bread through in the oven. Cut it in thick slices and rub each slice with the cut garlic glove. Trickle warm olive oil on to each slice. That's it!

Canapés of conserved tuna
Canapes de atún en conserva

Conserved tuna fish is a traditional larder-store all round the Mediterranean. The inshore fleet of Algeciras, for many years my local market-port, supplied a vigorous local tuna-canning industry until the recent depletion of stocks made the activity uneconomic.

Tuna is also salt-dried very much like cod, particularly round Valencia. The method yields *mojama* (middle-cut of tuna, salted and dried) and *huevas de mojama* (salted, dried roe). Both are expensive luxury tapas, served very thinly sliced and dressed with a trickle of olive oil.

Canned tuna is a more everyday pleasure. Serve the flaked, drained fish any way you please. Try it plain with bread and a small dish of olives (page 12), or dressed with a spoonful of mayonnaise (page 38) and a strip of red pepper. Or, as here, on lettuce leaves.

makes 8-10 tapa mouthfuls / serves 2 as a starter
200 g/7 oz can of tuna fish in olive oil
1 tablespoon finely chopped mild onion
1 tablespoon chopped parsley
8-10 bite-sized pieces of cos lettuce leaves
2-3 tablespoons olive oil
salt and pepper

Drain the tuna fish and flake it with the onion and parsley. Arrange the lettuce leaves on a plate.

Divide the tuna between the lettuce leaves. Dress with a trickle of oil and a sprinkle of salt and pepper.

Salt cod with chilli
Pericana

Bacalao (salt cod) was an essential store cupboard item throughout the Mediterranean during the Middle Ages, when Roman Catholics observed more than half the year as fasting. It remains popular even when fresh fish is on offer. This is a dish from the shepherding villages in the mountains behind Valencia, where *bacalao* is called 'mountain fish'. Choose firm white salt cod without any yellow tinge – the middle cut is the best. *Pericana* should be served with a *coca*, a Valencian unleavened bread much like pitta.

makes 15-20 tapa mouthfuls / serves 4 as a starter

250 g/8 oz salt cod, soaked in fresh water for 48 hours to de-salt
½ head of garlic
2 red sweet peppers (or dried red sweet peppers, deep-fried)
2 tablespoons olive oil
1 level teaspoon hot pimentón or powdered chilli
2-3 unleavened breads (pitta or nan, to replace coca), to serve

Dry the salt cod well, remove any bones, and trim it into manageable pieces for grilling (broiling).

Carefully hold the head of garlic in a direct flame with tongs and burn off the papery outside. Peel the cloves. Turn the peppers in the flame until the skin blisters black. Skin, hull and de-seed the peppers.

Heat a heavy iron pan (skillet) or griddle until it is smoking hot. Put on the garlic cloves. Blister the salt cod on a high heat, turning once, until its edges blacken.

Skin the cod and tear it into small flakes with the fingers – no nonsense with knives. Tear the peppers into strips. Chop the garlic. Toss all the ingredients together. Sprinkle with the olive oil and a little cayenne pepper to add extra bite. Leave to infuse for half an hour or so.

Accompany with hot pitta or any unleavened bread.

Canned sardines with onion
Sardinas en conserva con cebolla

Sardines are an excellent instant tapa, served plain or mashed with a little mayonnaise (page 38), spread on toast and topped with a strip of pimento. I like them on grilled bread with a little onion to cut the oiliness of the fish. A standard small can of sardines contains three to five fish.

makes 6-10 tapa mouthfuls / serves 2 as a starter
120 g/4 oz can of sardines in olive oil
sweet onion, sliced finely
6-8 smallish slices bread, toasted or grilled (broiled)
a little more olive oil (optional)
salt and pepper

Fillet the sardines horizontally. Remove the backbone if you prefer (I like its crunchiness).

Lay a few rings of onion on each piece of bread. Rural Spanish housewives toast bread on a metal plate topped with a hinged grill set over a direct flame. The process gives deliciously charred soft toast, rather than the smooth all-over tan of a toaster.

Top the onion with half a sardine, skin-side up. Sprinkle with salt and pepper, the oil from the can and a trickle of extra oil, if wished.

SALADS
AND COLD DISHES

A wide variety of cold dishes and substantial salads are the mainstay of the tapa table all over Spain. Less varied than the hot dishes, they back up the specialities of the house. They serve a double function: ready-prepared, they can be served immediately; in addition they offer an economical vehicle for the surplus from the restaurant. At home, these little salads can be made with small quantities of left-overs, and the advance preparation they require makes them ideal cold starters to a meal.

In the tapa bar, there are a few old favourites without which no selection would be considered complete. These vary from region to region, but in the south they include a cold potato tortilla (page 94), fresh-pickled anchovies, dressed artichoke hearts, and egg mayonnaise.

Cold cooked vegetables are transformed as a mayonnaise-coated Russian salad (very popular as a free tapa) or in a potato salad. Most bars offer a mixed fish salad dressed with oil and vinegar – a dish which accommodates any ready-cooked shellfish and crustaceans which remain unsold at the end of the day, and whose flavour is enhanced by a night's marination.

Any of these dishes, alone or in combination, make excellent first courses. Two or three served together with a green salad make a light summer lunch.

Opposite: Russian Salad

Russian salad with mayonnaise
Ensalada rusa a la mahonesa

This is the standby of every tapa bar, and it's often dressed with homemade mayonnaise. The making of this famous sauce is a skill which comes easily to Spanish housewives, who maintain that it has its origins in Mahon, Menorca. It cannot be made in really small quantities – a one-egg-yolk sauce is the minimum. Store any extra in a screw-top jar in the fridge, and, once it has cooled, don't beat it again even if it looks like separating.

You can, of course, use ready-cooked vegetables in the dish, and vary the combinations. Once made, it keeps for at least two to three days in a covered container in the fridge.

makes 15-20 tapa mouthfuls / serves 2 as a starter

the vegetables
1 large carrot, diced small
1 small turnip, diced small
1 large potato, diced small
2 tablespoons green beans, cut into short lengths
2 tablespoons shelled peas
1 tablespoon wine vinegar
1 tablespoon olive oil
salt

the mayonnaise
1 egg yolk
150 ml/¼ pint/⅔ cup olive oil
1 tablespoon sherry or wine vinegar
salt

to serve
lettuce leaves (optional)

Cook the vegetables in boiling salted water, adding them in the order in which they are listed. As soon as they are soft (8-10 minutes for the carrot and turnip which need longest), drain and splash them under cold water. Coat them with the vinegar and oil and a little salt.

Make the mayonnaise while the vegetables cool. Put the egg yolk in a deep plate and beat it with a fork. Very slowly trickle in the oil, drop by drop at first, beating steadily with the fork. As the sauce thickens, so you can increase the trickle – if the egg yolk is small, it will not accept all the oil. If it looks like splitting, fork furiously at one little corner until you get the sauce smooth and thick again, and then work in the rest. Finish with the vinegar and a little salt.

Alternatively, make the mayonnaise in a food processor, using the egg white as well as the egg yolk.

Turn the cooled vegetables in enough mayonnaise to coat them. Serve a teaspoonful in individual saucers with forks, or in small lettuce leaves.

Potato mayonnaise with red sweet peppers
Patatas a la mahonesa

This simple salad is delicious made with leftover baked potatoes. A few chopped gherkins make a good addition, and the red sweet pepper can be replaced with a sprinkle of pimentón (the same vegetable dried and ground to a powder). This dish can be prepared two or three days in advance and kept in a covered container in the fridge.

makes 12-15 tapa mouthfuls / serves 2 as a starter
2 large cooked potatoes, skinned and diced
2 tablespoons olive oil
1 teaspoon sherry or wine vinegar
3-4 tablespoons mayonnaise (page 38)
2-3 strips of red sweet pepper
salt and pepper
small lettuce leaves, to serve (optional)

Toss the diced potatoes with the oil, vinegar, and salt and pepper – best done while the potatoes are still hot. When the potatoes are quite cool, coat them with the mayonnaise and decorate with the strips of red sweet pepper.

Serve the potato mayonnaise either in individual saucers with forks, or spooned into small lettuce leaves – these make neat edible containers for sloppy tapas.

Eggs with mayonnaise
Huevos con mahonesa

This is a favourite of tapa bars. The quality is dependent upon the raw materials – if the mayonnaise is homemade, and the eggs just gathered from underneath a barnyard hen, there is no finer dish.

makes 16 tapa mouthfuls / serves 4 as a starter

4 medium eggs
4 tablespoons mayonnaise (page 38)
1-2 strips of cooked red pepper or 1 teaspoon pimentón

Start the eggs in cold water and bring them gently to the boil. Take the pan off the heat, lid it and leave them in the water for 6-8 minutes to set the yolks. Plunge the eggs into cold water to loosen the shell. Peel them, halve them and arrange them on a plate.

Dress each egg-half with ½ teaspoon of the mayonnaise and a scrap of the red pepper or a pinch of pimentón. (This is the moment when the icing nozzle usually comes into play in the grander tapa bars.)

If serving as a first course, the eggs can be presented on a large dish. For a tapa, serve each egg-half cut in half again and speared with a cocktail stick.

Note: the yolks can be taken out and mashed up with a little oil, a pinch of ground cumin and an anchovy or two if you are not perfectly confident that your eggs are of the best.

Prawns with mayonnaise
Cóctel de gambas

The ubiquitous prawn cocktail turns up regularly on the Spanish menu. Since it combines Spain's two great culinary strengths – excellent fresh shellfish and homemade mayonnaise – it can be very good. This version comes from the Campo de Gibraltar, where Worcestershire sauce has long been a favourite in the local bars. Make it up as you need it – this is not a dish which keeps well.

makes 8-10 tapa mouthfuls / serves 2 as a starter
125 g/4 oz cooked peeled prawns
3 tablespoons mayonnaise (page 38)
½ teaspoon paprika
1 teaspoon Worcestershire sauce
1 teaspoon tomato purée
1 teaspoon gin
salt and pepper
lettuce leaves or cherry tomatoes, to serve

Pick over the prawns and drain them thoroughly if they were frozen. Combine the mayonnaise with the paprika, Worcestershire sauce, tomato purée and gin. Taste and adjust the seasoning if necessary. Dress the prawns with this sauce.

Serve spooned into small lettuce leaves or tiny hollowed-out tomatoes, each speared with a cocktail stick.

Cherry tomatoes mimosa
Tomatitos a la mimosa

This is a quickly prepared tapa which takes advantage of those tiny cherry tomatoes which might have been specially grown for the purpose. It's just as good, although not as pretty, made with the larger ones. This can be assembled a few hours ahead.

makes 8-10 tapa mouthfuls / serves 2 as a starter
8-10 cherry tomatoes
1 hard-boiled egg
2-3 anchovy fillets
8 green olive slices
1-2 tablespoons olive oil

Cut the top off each little tomato and, with a sharp-edged teaspoon, scoop out the soft middle including the seeds. Chop the egg finely. Chop the anchovies with the tomato tops.

Stuff the tomato shells with the anchovy mixture, top with the olive slices, and finish with the chopped hard-boiled egg and trickle of the olive oil. Spear each tomato with a cocktail stick before serving.

Cod's roe salad
Ensalada de huevas de merluza

This is one of my favourite tapa-salads. Cod's roe and hake roe (*huevas de merluza*) look and cook alike, but in Spain hake is more usual. The dressing is also good on leftover cooked mussels and other shellfish. It keeps for four to five days in the fridge.

makes 12-15 tapa mouthfuls /
serves 2 as a starter
1 wing of cooked cod's roe
1 tablespoon chopped spring onion
1 tablespoon chopped red sweet pepper
1 garlic clove, chopped
1 teaspoon chopped parsley
3-4 tablespoons olive oil
1 tablespoon sherry or wine vinegar
salt and pepper

Skin and dice the cod's roe into 1 cm (½ inch) cubes. Mix the rest of the ingredients together and pour them over the roe. Turn the pieces gently in the marinade, taking care not to break them up. Leave in a cool place or the fridge to marinate for a few hours or overnight.

Serve one piece of roe per tapa portion, with a little of the marinade poured over and plenty of bread to mop up the juices.

Vinegar-pickled anchovies
Boquerones en vinagre

The fresh anchovy looks like a small slender sardine: both fish are a plentiful catch on the southern coasts of Spain. In pre-refrigeration days, a salt-and-vinegar bath provided a simple method of adding a little shelf-life to small fish which couldn't be eaten fresh. The preparation was so good it has remained on the tapa menu ever since. Start forty-eight hours ahead – maybe when *you* have a handful of fish left over from frying (page 115). The preparation keeps for four to five days in the fridge.

makes 10-12 tapa mouthfuls / serves 2 as a starter
250 g/8 oz fresh anchovies or sprats
1-2 garlic cloves, sliced
4 tablespoons sherry or wine vinegar
1 tablespoon olive oil
pinch chopped parsley
salt and pepper

Rinse the anchovies – they have no scales to worry about; sprats will have to be checked for scales. Gut the little fish with your finger through the soft belly. Pull the head of each fish firmly down through the belly towards the tail. This will bring the spine with it and leave the fish split in a butterfly, all in one movement. Otherwise, cut the fish in half with a sharp knife and remove the backbone.

Lay the butterflied fish flesh-side up in a single layer in a shallow

dish. Sprinkle with the garlic, and salt and pepper. Mix the vinegar with its own volume of water (sherry vinegar is powerful stuff) and pour it over the fish.

Cover with foil and leave in the fridge to marinate for 48 hours. Before serving, drain away the salty juices and trickle the fish with a little olive oil and a sprinkle of parsley.

Serve one fish per tapa, with a chunk of bread and cocktail sticks.

Asparagus with two sauces
Espárragos con dos salsas

Mayonnaise and fresh-flavoured chopped-vegetable sauce often turn up as an accompaniment to grilled fish steaks. The vegetable sauce was a particular favourite in my local bar in Tarifa, where it seemed to appear with everything, including a bit of bread for dunking; in the winter it sauced a baked potato.

makes 8 tapa mouthfuls / serves 1 as a starter
8 cooked asparagus spears, well-drained and cooled
2-3 tablespoons mayonnaise (page 38)
chopped vegetable sauce
1 small tomato, chopped finely
½ green pepper, chopped finely
2-3 cocktail gherkins, chopped finely
½ onion, chopped finely
1 tablespoon chopped parsley
4 tablespoons olive oil
2 tablespoons sherry or wine vinegar
1 garlic clove, chopped finely (optional)
salt and pepper

Trim off the woody ends of the asparagus.

Mix together all the ingredients for the chopped vegetable sauce.

Serve each asparagus spear flanked with a teaspoon of mayonnaise and a teaspoon of chopped vegetable sauce.

Red sweet peppers in oil
Pimientos en aceite

This preparation is worth making in larger quantities as it keeps for a couple of weeks in the fridge. It's my own favourite larder standby – not only is it delicious on its own, it is also very useful for decorating other tapas. Store it in a screw-top jar, topped up with olive oil so that the peppers are submerged. Any leftover oil is delicious trickled over a potato salad, or used in a seafood mayonnaise.

makes 12-15 tapa mouthfuls / serves 2 as a starter

2 large red sweet peppers
6 tablespoons olive oil
1 garlic clove, sliced
cubes of bread, to serve

Hull and de-seed the peppers and cut them into strips.

Heat the oil till just before it bubbles in a small frying pan (skillet). Add the peppers and stew them gently until they are soft and the juices have evaporated so that the oil is once again clear and the edges of the peppers begin to brown. (As the oil heats up, the sugar in the peppers caramelises, which gives the finished dish a lovely roasted flavour.) Throw in the garlic at the last minute – it should soften but not brown. Take the peppers off the heat, and tip the contents of the pan into a small dish to cool.

Cut the pepper strips into bite-sized pieces. Serve them in their garlic-flavoured oil, speared on to cubes of bread with cocktail sticks. This is the most delectable of finger-food.

Artichokes in oil
Alcachofas en aceite

This is a very common tapa in the south of Spain, where artichokes are plentiful and cheap. It can be made with canned artichoke hearts.

makes 4 tapa portions / serves 2 as a starter

**4 small cooked artichokes or artichoke hearts
6 tablespoons olive oil
1 garlic clove, chopped finely
1 spring onion, chopped finely
salt and pepper**

Arrange the artichokes on a deep plate into which you have trickled a little of the oil. If the artichokes are whole, trim the leaves right down to the tender base without pulling them away, and carefully cut out the choke (the nest of hairy little leaves at the heart).

Mix the garlic and spring onion with the remaining oil, and salt and pepper. Pour this dressing into the artichoke hearts.

Note: finely chopped peppers, egg, tomato or cucumber can be mixed into the dressing if you have any left over from another tapa dish.

New potato salad
Ensalada de patatas frescas

This is my household's favourite summer lunch – a conveniently pre-cooked feast which sits in a large dish on the table all day for the sustenance of passing hungry teenagers. The leftovers make good little tapas in the evening.

makes 20-24 tapa mouthfuls / serves 2 as a light main course

**500 g/1 lb new potatoes, cooked in their skins
4 tablespoons olive oil**

1 tablespoon sherry or wine vinegar
1 tablespoon diced cucumber
1 tablespoon diced green pepper
1 tablespoon diced red sweet pepper
1 tablespoon chopped onion (spring onion is excellent)
1 hard-boiled egg, chopped roughly
3-4 anchovy fillets, chopped
6-8 black olives
salt and pepper

Toss the potatoes with the oil, vinegar, and salt and pepper while they're still hot. When the potatoes have cooled a little, mix in the rest of the ingredients.

For a more substantial main-course dish, top just before serving with diced bread fried crisp in olive oil with garlic.

Serve with forks in individual dishes or on one large serving plate.

Rice salad with pine kernels
Ensalada de arroz can piñones

Prepared in larger quantities, this Valencian rice salad is excellent with cold chicken or ham. If serving it to accompany a meal, allow 75 g/3 oz/$\frac{1}{2}$ cup uncooked weight of rice per person (double these quantities for cooked rice).

makes 15-20 tapa mouthfuls /
serves 3-4 as a starter or to accompany cold meat

8 heaped tablespoons cooked rice
1 tablespoon toasted pine kernels or slivered almonds
1 tablespoon cooked peas
1 tablespoon chopped apple or celery
1 tablespoon chopped green pepper
1 tablespoon chopped red sweet pepper
3 tablespoons olive oil

1 tablespoon lemon juice
salt
chicory leaves, to serve (optional)

Toss all the ingredients lightly together. Serve in individual saucers with small forks. Alternatively, serve spooned into chicory leaves (conveniently boat-shaped), with a cocktail stick speared into each.

Beetroot salad
Ensalada de remolacha

Look for fresh-cooked beetroot which hasn't been sodden in vinegar for this fresh-flavoured salad. There is no salt or vinegar in the seasoning – the garlic gives it enough bite. It can be prepared a day or two ahead and left to marinate in the fridge.

makes 12-15 tapa mouthfuls / serves 2 as a starter
250 g/8 oz cooked beetroot, skinned and diced
1 garlic clove, chopped
1 tablespoon chopped parsley
2 tablespoons olive oil pepper

Spread the diced beetroot in a flat dish in a single layer. Sprinkle over the rest of the ingredients. Leave to marinate for an hour or two, or overnight.

Serve with cocktail sticks or forks for easy handling.

Chicory stuffed with blue cheese
Ojas de chicoria con queso de cabrales

This is a very common tapa in the north of Spain, where the French influence is strong. The boat-shaped leaves of endive (also known as chicory or white-leaf) make perfect finger-food. The stuffing, while other blue-veins will do, is usually the pungent Cabrales, a blue-vein made in Asturias in much the same way as Roquefort.

makes 8 tapa mouthfuls / serves 2 as a starter
8 boat-shaped chicory (endive) leaves
125 g/4 oz blue-veined cheese (Cabrales for preference)
2 tablespoons soured cream
1 teaspoon mild or hot pimentón (smoked for preference)

Wipe the chicory leaves and arrange them on a plate. Mash the cheese with the soured cream.

Stuff the leaves with the cheese mixture. Finish with a sprinkle of pimentón and a cocktail stick for easy handling.

Rice salad with tuna fish
Ensalada de arroz can atún en conserva

Leftover rice is the basis for this salad. In Spain the usual rice is round – similar to our pudding rice. Long-grain rice will do as well. It's a good standby for a buffet – particularly to accompany cold seafood such as prawns, lobster or salmon with mayonnaise. For a full portion, allow about 75 g/3 oz/¼ cup uncooked weight of rice per person (double these quantities for cooked rice).

makes 15-20 tapa mouthfuls /
serves 3-4 as a starter or to accompany seafood
8 heaped tablespoons cooked rice

1 tablespoon chopped green pepper
1 tablespoon chopped onion
1 tablespoon chopped cucumber
1 tablespoon chopped parsley
1 tablespoon flaked tuna fish
4 tablespoons olive oil
1 tablespoon lemon juice
salt and pepper
small lettuce leaves, to serve (optional)

Toss all the ingredients lightly together and serve in little dishes with forks, or spooned into small lettuce leaves.

Salad kebabs
Pinchos de ensalada mixta

The Spanish mixed salad is as variable as the market garden can make it. Apart from artichoke hearts, it doesn't usually include cooked vegetables – they go into *ensalada rusa* (page 38). Otherwise, anything goes. It makes an excellent start to a summer meal – a kind of Spanish *salade niçoise*. When serving it as a tapa, spear the ingredients, kebab-style, on a cocktail stick to make a *pincho*.

makes 16 tapa mouthfuls / serves 2 as a starter
2-3 cos lettuce leaves, sliced across the stalk
1 small tomato, cut into 8
8 small cubes of cucumber
8 anchovy-stuffed green olives
1 slice of mild onion or 1 spring onion,
cut into pieces
1 cooked artichoke heart, cut into 8
1 small red sweet or green pepper, hulled, deseeded
and chopped into 8

1 hard-boiled egg, chopped finely
3 tablespoons olive oil
a squeeze of lemon juice
salt

Thread the lettuce, tomato, cucumber, olives, onion, artichoke and pepper on to 8 cocktail sticks, kebab-style. Dress with the chopped hard-boiled egg, oil, lemon juice and a little salt.

Tomatoes with anchovies
Tomates con anchoas

This is a classic combination in Spain. Salt-cured anchovies are still sold straight from the barrel in Andalucían markets and elsewhere. If bought loose, the whiskery little fish have to be boned and soaked in milk before using – canned ones are much easier.

makes 8-10 tapa mouthfuls / serves 2 as a starter
1 large ripe beef tomato, sliced
1 can of anchovies in oil (8-10 fillets)
8-10 pimento-stuffed olives

Arrange the tomato slices on a plate in a single layer. Roll the anchovy fillets and place one on each slice. Top each with a stuffed olive and a trickle of oil from the can.

Tomatoes with garlic and marjoram
Tomates con ajo y mejorana

Choose a ripe tomato and firm fresh garlic for this simple combination: its success depends on good raw materials freshly prepared. Onion and parsley can be substituted for the marjoram and garlic.

makes 8-10 tapa mouthfuls / serves 1-2 as a starter

1 large ripe beef tomato
1 garlic clove
1 teaspoon marjoram leaves
1-2 tablespoons olive oil
a pinch of granulated sugar
pepper

Wipe and slice the tomato. Arrange the slices on a plate in a single layer. Slice the garlic very finely and scatter over the tomatoes. Trickle with the olive oil and finish with marjoram leaves, pepper and a sprinkle of sugar.

Red pepper and tuna casserole
Pote

I first tasted this delicious combination of roasted red peppers and preserved tuna in Mora de Toledo in La Mancha – where they grow the finest and juiciest of sweet red peppers. Mora is a little white-washed town set in the red earth of the central plateau's olive groves. The harvest is late up on the high plain, production small but quality high – particularly the greeny-gold first-pressing virgin oils. This dish can be prepared a day or two ahead.

makes 10-12 tapa mouthfuls / serves 2 as a starter

2 large red salad peppers
6 tablespoons virgin olive oil

1-2 garlic cloves, crushed
1 teaspoon dried thyme leaves
1 hard-boiled egg, sliced
200 g/7 oz can of tuna fish in oil, drained and flaked
freshly-ground pepper

Preheat the oven to Gas Mark 8/230°C/450°F.

Using a long toasting fork carefully blister the peppers over a direct flame, or under the grill, until the skin blackens and peels off easily (drop into a plastic bag to loosen stubborn patches). Hull and deseed the peppers and slice the flesh into thick strips.

Trickle a little of the oil into 2 small shallow earthenware casseroles – cazuelas – or 1 larger baking dish, and lay in the strips of pepper. Trickle with the rest of the oil.

Cook in the oven for 15-20 minutes until the peppers are sizzling. Sprinkle with the garlic and thyme and leave to cool.

When you are ready to serve, sprinkle with slices of hard-boiled egg, tuna-flakes and a turn of the pepper-grinder.

Serve with chunks of bread and little forks for sharing from the cooking dish.

Seafood salad
Ensalada de mariscos

The ingredients for this vary with the local catch. All shellfish and crustaceans (except crab, which is not firm enough) are welcome. Make up your own combinations. If these are lacking, increase the proportion of cucumber and green pepper and add a few cubes of cold potato. It makes a good first course, served on shredded lettuce.

makes 20-24 tapa mouthfuls / serves 4 as a starter
2 tablespoons prawns, cooked and peeled (fresh or frozen)
2 tablespoons clams or cockles, cooked and shelled
(fresh or canned)
2 tablespoons mussels, cooked and shelled
2 tablespoons cooked, sliced squid
1 tablespoon diced green pepper
1 tablespoon diced cucumber
1 tablespoon diced onion
1 tablespoon chopped parsley
5 tablespoons olive oil
2 tablespoons sherry or wine vinegar
½ teaspoon crushed coriander seeds
salt and pepper
To serve (optional)
small crisp lettuce leaves

Combine all the ingredients and leave them to marinate overnight.
Serve either in small individual dishes with forks, or heaped on lettuce leaves spiked with cocktail sticks.

VEGETABLES

Spain has an excellent choice of good vegetables. Markets are particularly strong, of course, in Mediterranean varieties that need plenty of sunshine to ripen to perfection – peppers, aubergines (eggplants), artichokes and tomatoes among them.

All our own familiar northern vegetables grow very well in the fertile climate and make their appearance on the tapa table, including green beans and broad beans, potatoes and carrots, and leeks and onions. Less familiar vegetables include a variety of wild greens for example *tagarninas* – the leaf-rosettes of a tall yellow-flowered thistle – and the thin shoots of wild or naturalised asparagus; and in winter Swiss chard and cardoons (a winter-maturing member of the artichoke family). Spaniards – with the exception of the Basques and Catalans – are wary of their wild fungi, preferring the more reliable cultivated variety labelled Paris mushrooms, *champiñon de Paris*, for the caves just outside the French capital in which the field-mushroom was first cultivated. Varieties considered trustworthy include porcini mushrooms (*setas*), a variety of oyster mushroom parasitic on members of the artichoke family (*cardoncello*), and the orange-tear or saffron milkcap, a pine-wood fungi which bruises blue and weeps milky tears when cut.

Vegetables in Spain are often served separately at the beginning of the meal. Any of the following recipes make a delicious first course.

Opposite: Grilled mushrooms with garlic and rosemary

Grilled (broiled) mushrooms with garlic and rosemary
Champiñones a la parrilla

I have included rosemary in this recipe to give the flavour of the Andalucían *maquis* (scrub-covered hills), where mushrooms are a wild-gathered crop in autumn and spring. As well as the usual damp meadows, they seem to spring up in the charred wake of forest fires.

makes 8 tapa mouthfuls / serves 2 as a starter
250 g/8 oz mushrooms (flat or well-grown buttons)
1-2 fat garlic cloves
1 teaspoon dried rosemary
2 tablespoons olive oil
salt and pepper
bread squares, to serve

Wipe the mushrooms and trim the stalks level with the caps. Discard the trimmings. Arrange the mushrooms stalk upwards on a grill (broiling) pan or griddle.

Chop the garlic finely. Sprinkle the mushroom caps with the chopped garlic, rosemary, olive oil and salt and pepper.

Grill (broil) the mushrooms fiercely until the juices run and the caps are spitting hot. Serve on squares of fresh bread, each speared with a cocktail stick (see photo page 63).

Baked potatoes with oil and onion
Patatas con cebolla

A substantial tapa for a cold winter evening; this dish is from the mountains of Huesca.

makes 4 large tapa portions / serves 4 as a starter
4 medium-size potatoes
1 mild onion (Spanish), chopped finely
6 tablespoons olive oil
salt and pepper

Preheat the oven to Gas Mark 5/190°C/375°F.

Scrub the potatoes and bake them in the oven for an hour, until the flesh is soft and the skin crisp.

Mix the chopped onion with the olive oil and salt and pepper.

Open up the potatoes and spoon in the oil and onion mixture. Eat them hot, one each per tapa.

Baked porcini mushrooms with parsley and garlic
Setas al homo

This simple recipe can be also used for any wild fungi of suitable size and cap-shape, though the larger porcini would have to be sliced. In the tapa-bars of Valencia and Barcelona it's the favourite way with saffron milkcaps.

makes 8-10 tapa mouthfuls / serves 2 as a starter
About 250 g/8 oz smallish open-cap mushrooms
4 tablespoons olive oil
1 garlic clove, chopped
1 heaped tablespoon chopped parsley
2 heaped tablespoons fresh breadcrumbs
salt and pepper

Preheat the oven to Gas Mark 6/200°C/400°F.

Wipe the mushrooms and trim off the stalks close to the caps. Arrange the caps in a shallow ovenproof dish which will just accommodate them. Chop the stalks and tuck them into the gaps. Trickle the oil over and around the mushrooms and sprinkle them with salt and pepper. Bake in the oven for 20-25 minutes.

Meanwhile fork the garlic, parsley and breadcrumbs lightly together. After the mushrooms have been cooking for 10 minutes, top them with the mixture. Baste the topping with the mushroom juices and return the dish to the oven for the remaining 10-15 minutes.

Serve the mushrooms sizzling hot, if possible in their cooking dish.

Fried green peppers
Pimientos fritos

Mediterranean housewives can choose specially-grown, thin-fleshed green Padrón peppers for frying. If you can find them, buy them for this dish. It can be made with the widely available thick-fleshed variety – which in Spain would be used for stuffing or in salads – but they must be cut into strips for frying.

makes 8 tapa mouthfuls / serves 2 as a starter

**8 small thin-fleshed green peppers or 2 large
thick-fleshed sweet red or green peppers
4 tablespoons olive oil
Sea salt**

If the peppers are the small thin-fleshed variety, wipe them and leave them whole. If you have the thick-fleshed peppers hull, de-seed and cut them into finger-width (1.5 cm/½ inch) strips.

Heat the oil in a frying pan (skillet) until a faint blue haze rises. Throw in the peppers. Cook them fiercely but briefly, turning until all sides take a little colour. Sprinkle with a little salt, turn the heat right down and lid the pan. Cook over a gentle heat until the peppers are soft.

Take out the peppers and arrange them in a dish. Serve them hot or cold, sauced with their own cooking juices, with plenty of bread to mop up the aromatic oil.

Aubergine (eggplant) fritters
Berejenas fritas

This tapa is quickly prepared, cheap and delicious. What more can anyone ask? The same technique can be applied to courgettes (zucchini). In my family the fritters vanish as soon as they come out of the pan.

makes 10-12 tapa mouthfuls / serves 2 as a starter,
with a fresh tomato sauce (page 176)
1 large aubergine (eggplant)
2 tablespoons milk
2 tablespoons plain (all purpose) flour
1 teaspoon paprika
oil for shallow-frying
salt

Wipe and hull the aubergine (eggplant) and cut it into thin slices. Salt the slices and put them in a colander to drain for half an hour (I don't always do this, but it is traditional). Rinse and pat dry.

Pour the milk on to a flat plate. Spread the flour on to another plate and mix in the paprika.

Heat a finger's width (1.5 cm/½ inch) of oil in a frying pan (skillet). When it hazes with blue smoke, dip the slices of aubergine (eggplant) first in the milk and then in the flour, and then slip them into the hot oil. Fry them to a crisp. Transfer to kitchen paper to drain.

Continue until all the aubergine (eggplant) is done. Serve the fritters immediately.

Aubergine (eggplant) purée
Pez de tierra

The Spanish name for this purée is 'earth fish'. I had it first in Peñiscola, where the last of the Avignon Popes spent his final days. It's a

fast-day dish, meatless, a matter of importance in Catholic Spain where, in medieval times, the designation applied to more than half the year. The ingredients were considerably cheaper than *pez de monte* – mountain fish – the nickname given to the alternative fasting-food, *bacalao* (salt cod).

makes 10-12 tapa mouthfuls / serves 2 as a starter
1 large firm aubergine (eggplant)
3 garlic cloves
6 tablespoons olive oil
½ teaspoon ground cumin
salt and pepper

Wipe, hull and cut the aubergine (eggplant) into chunks – don't bother with the salting and rinsing so often advocated. Chop the garlic roughly.

Heat the oil in a shallow pan (skillet). Add the garlic and cook it for a minute or two. Add the chunked aubergine (eggplant). Fry, turning as each side cooks, until the aubergine (eggplant) is soft – about 10 minutes over a medium heat.

Pour the contents of the pan into a food processor or liquidiser, with the seasoning and the cumin, and reduce it all to a speckled purée. This can also be done the traditional way with a pestle and mortar.

Serve the purée warm, with chunks of bread for dipping.

Baked peppers and tomatoes
Asadillo

This is – or was – served as a tapa in the Venta del Quixote at Puerto Lapis near Aranjuez, La Mancha. It's delicious cold and keeps well in a screw-top jar in the fridge – just don't forget to bring it up to room temperature before serving.

makes 8-10 tapa mouthfuls / serves 2 as a starter
2 red sweet peppers
3 tablespoons olive oil
1 garlic clove, chopped
2 tomatoes, sliced
1 teaspoon dried marjoram or oregano
salt and pepper

Preheat the oven to Gas Mark 8/230°C/450°F.

Using a long toasting fork carefully roast the whole peppers over a gas flame, or under the grill, until the skin blisters black (the kitchen fills with the most delicious aroma). Hull, skin and de-seed the peppers. Cut them into strips.

Oil 4 individual shallow casseroles, or one larger one. Arrange the peppers, garlic and tomato in layers, seasoning as you go. Sprinkle with the rest of the oil and the marjoram or oregano. Bake in the oven for 20-25 minutes.

Serve hot in their dish or dishes, with bread for mopping.

Asparagus with soft-boiled eggs
Espárragos con huevos

This is a delicious version of nursery eggs. It is nicest made with the slender bright green stalks of sprue – wild-gathered asparagus – in Mediterranean countries. It can be made with the fat cultivated stalks if you prefer.

makes 12-18 tapa mouthfuls / serves 4 as a starter
A big handful (500 g/1 lb) thin green asparagus
4 medium eggs

to serve
olive oil
sea salt
bread

Wash and trim the asparagus. Tie them in a neat bundle and set them upright in a pan of boiling, salted water, so that the stalks are in water and the tops in steam only. Drain them when tender but not floppy – 3-4 minutes should do.

Soft-boil the eggs: start in cold water, bring gently to the boil, remove the pan from the heat, leave for 3 minutes, then remove the eggs from the water. Tap the round end to create a little balancing-shelf and halt the cooking-process.

Serve each person with a neatly-balanced egg (egg-cups don't happen in Spain unless you're a tourist) and hand the asparagus separately along with olive oil and sea salt and chunks of crusty bread for mopping.

Fried baby artichokes
Alcachofitas fritas

A very quick and easy way with the small leaf artichokes, no bigger than a baby's fist, which sometimes come our way at the beginning of the season in May and June. These juniors are sold tied by the stalk, in bundles of six to twelve. Only buy them if they have fresh tight heads like budding flowers. Mature artichokes can be prepared in this way, but the outside and tops of the leaves and the choke must be trimmed off first. This is my favourite tapa.

makes 24 tapa mouthfuls / serves 2 as a starter
6 baby artichokes
olive oil for shallow-frying
sea salt
1 lemon, quartered, to serve

Wipe the artichokes and trim the stalks off level with the base. With a sharp knife, peel off the rough outside of the stalks and cut them in half lengthways. Halve the artichokes and nick out the hairy little

choke.

In a frying pan (skillet) heat enough oil to half-submerge the artichokes when placed cut-side down in the pan. When a faint blue haze rises from the surface of the oil, put in as many artichoke halves as the pan will accommodate in a singe layer. Fry until the leaves are prettily bronzed and the choke tender, turning them once. Continue until all are ready, leaving the stalks till the end. Drain on kitchen paper, sprinkle with salt and serve with the quartered lemon. Eat them with your the fingers, from the choke towards the leaves, as far as is tender.

Broad beans with ham
Habas con jamón

Simple and quickly prepared, these quantities make an excellent little supper dish for one. Bacon is a closer approximation to the Spanish wind-dried hams than cooked ham. Any salt-cured raw ham is fine for this dish.

makes 10-12 tapa mouthfuls / serves 2 as a starter
250 g/8 oz shelled broad beans (fresh or frozen)
2 tablespoons olive oil
1-2 slices of lean bacon or salt-cured ham, chopped
1 tablespoon chopped parsley
salt and pepper

Blanch the beans in boiling, salted water for 2-3 minutes, unless they are old ones in which case they will need 6-10 minutes to become tender.

Warm the oil in a small pan. Add the chopped bacon or ham and fry it for a minute or two. Stir in the parsley and the beans. Lid and cook gently for 5 minutes. Taste and add salt and pepper.

Serve in small individual dishes or on a single plate with forks for each person.

Gratin of cardoons or chard stalks
Cardo o acelga gratinado

These two vegetables are particularly popular in winter in Spain, when there is not much else around. Cardoons are a member of the artichoke family, and their flavour is similar. I've had them served plain-boiled, dressed with olive oil and salt and pepper, and sometimes, as here, baked in a white sauce. Be careful, though, as the cardoon is very bitter unless it is properly trimmed of all its leaves. Chard is a good alternative, and easier to come by.

makes 18-20 tapa mouthfuls / serves 3-4 as a starter
3-4 inner stalks of cardoon or Swiss chard
1 tablespoon lemon juice or wine vinegar
2 tablespoons olive oil
1 heaped tablespoon plain (all-purpose) flour
1 tablespoon dry sherry
2 ladlesful ham or chicken stock
2 heaped tablespoons grated hard cheese
salt and pepper

If you are using cardoons, trim off the little fringe of leaf which edges the stalks, and discard the heart – all these are very bitter. If you use Swiss chard, use only the white stalks, and save the green leaves to use in the recipe for vinegar-dressed chard leaves on page 82.

Cut the stalks into bite-sized pieces and rinse them. Bring a pan of salted water to the boil. Add the lemon juice or vinegar and put in the cardoon or chard. Bring back to the boil, lid and cook for 20 minutes, until the stalks are tender. Drain well and arrange in a shallow gratin dish.

Meanwhile make the sauce. Warm the oil in a small pan. Stir in the flour and cook for a moment to mix the two. Add the sherry. Pour in the rest of the liquid gradually, whisking to avoid lumps till you have a smooth runny sauce. Cook gently until the sauce is thick enough to coat the back of the spoon. Beat in half the cheese. Taste and add salt and pepper.

Pour the sauce over and around the cooked vegetables. Sprinkle with the rest of the grated cheese and slide the dish under the grill to melt and brown the cheese.

New potatoes with garlic and saffron
Patatas frescas en ajopollo

The Moors, who colonised Andalucía for five centuries, left their mark on Spanish cuisine. Potatoes are given a Moorish treatment in this dish from Malaga. It makes a delicious first course. The dish can be prepared in advance up to the final reduction of the sauce.

makes about 8 tapa mouthfuls / serves 2 as a starter

2 generous handfuls small new potatoes
2 tablespoons olive oil
1 tablespoon fresh breadcrumbs
1 garlic clove, crushed
6 blanched almonds
1 tablespoon chopped parsley
6-8 saffron threads infused in a little boiling water
2 tablespoons water
salt and pepper

Scrub the potatoes well but leave them whole.

Heat the oil in a small frying pan (skillet). Fry the breadcrumbs, garlic and almonds in the oil until all are lightly golden. Tip the contents of the pan into a liquidiser or processor. Add the parsley and saffron with its soaking-water and process to a paste – or use a pestle and mortar.

Put the potatoes into a small saucepan with enough water to cover. Bring to the boil, stir in the paste, season with salt and pepper, lid the pan and simmer gently until the potatoes are perfectly tender – about 15 minutes. Take off the lid and boil rapidly, shaking the pan to break the potato skins a little, until the cooking-liquid is reduced to a dressing rather than a sauce.

French fries
Patatas fritas

This is the easiest and most delicious of tapas – well worth the effort of making your own. Triple-cooking the potatoes in olive oil – use one of the cheaper non-virgins – ensures crispness as well as flavour, and you can always re-use the oil.

makes 30-40 French fries
**3-4 large old potatoes
olive oil for frying (about 600 ml/1 pint/2½ cups)
salt**

Wash, peel and slice the potatoes. Cut them into chips about the length and width of your index finger.

Heat the oil in a small enough pan to give you a depth of about two fingers' width (3 cm/1 inch). When the surface is lightly hazed with blue, slip in a handful of chips – not too many to avoid dropping the oil-temperature below a rapid bubble.

Bring the oil back to the boil, turn down the heat and cook gently until the potato is just tender but has not yet taken colour. Transfer to a colander set over a bowl to catch the drippings. Continue till all are ready.

Return the drippings to the pan and reheat till bubbles no longer rise. Add the chips in batches as before, this time salting lightly when the potato hits the oil, and cook till pale gold and beginning to crisp. Remove to the colander to drain.

Repeat the frying process, this time making sure the oil is very hot so that the potato browns and crisps immediately. Transfer to the colander – this time lined with kitchen paper – pat to remove excess oil, and serve immediately.

Re-fried cauliflower with garlic
Coliflor al ajo arriero

This dish is a weakness of mine, not least because it makes a fine supper when I'm on my own (well, maybe topped out with a fried egg). It's just as good cold as hot.

makes 15-18 tapa mouthfuls / serves 2 as a starter

1 small cauliflower
3-4 tablespoons olive oil
2-3 garlic cloves, chopped
1 teaspoon cumin seeds
1 teaspoon hot pimentón (or chilli powder)
1 tablespoon chopped parsley
1 tablespoon sherry or wine vinegar
salt

Wash the cauliflower and divide it into bite-sized florets. Cook it in boiling, salted water until soft – about 15 minutes. Drain.

Heat the oil in a frying pan (skillet). Turn the garlic in the hot oil until it softens and takes a little colour. Sprinkle in the cumin seeds and fry for a minute or two to release the aroma. Add the cauliflower, mash to break it up a little, and sprinkle with the pimentón or chilli. Continue to fry gently for 10 minutes or so, turning it regularly, until the florets brown a little. Transfer to a serving dish and sprinkle with the parsley, vinegar and salt.

Serve hot or cold, with forks for everyone.

Peppery potatoes
Patatas bravas

Recipes for this simple combination of a fiery scarlet sauce with plain-cooked potatoes (fried or baked or boiled) are as varied as the tapa-bars which serve them. The original, it's said, was invented in a bar in Barcelona, though there are many who claim the honour. The cheaper establishments in Spain are very inventive with potatoes.

makes 10-12 tapa mouthfuls / serves 2 as a starter

2 large old potatoes
4-5 tablespoons olive oil
1 tablespoon mild pimentón (smoked, for preference)
1 teaspoon hot pimentón
salt

Preheat the oven to Gas Mark 8/230°C/450°F. Alternatively, the cooking can be done on the top of the cooker – either in a heavy frying pan (skillet), or in a casserole which will resist direct heat.

Peel the potatoes and cut them into thick wedges. Pour half the oil into 4 individual shallow earthenware casseroles or a small gratin dish, transfer to the oven and wait until the oil is smoking.

Arrange the potatoes in the hot oil in a single layer. Trickle on the rest of the oil, sprinkle with salt and return to the oven. Cook the potatoes until soft inside and crisp on the outside – this will take 25-35 minutes.

Mix the hot and mild pimentón and sprinkle over the potatoes. Serve them hot in their cooking dish.

Potatoes with pepper and tomato sauce
Machacón

This cheap-and-cheerful dish from La Mancha is made with baked potatoes in the winter – and the winters in La Mancha are harsh – and new potatoes in summer. This is the hot-weather version.

makes 8-10 tapa mouthfuls / serves 2 as a starter

250 g/8 oz small new potatoes
1 tablespoon chopped green pepper
1 large tomato, skinned and chopped
1 tablespoon chopped cucumber
2 tablespoons lemon juice
2-3 tablespoons olive oil
1 teaspoon cumin seeds, dry-roasted and crushed
salt and pepper

Scrub and cook the new potatoes in boiling, salted water until soft – about 15 minutes, depending on size. Drain them thoroughly.

Mix the chopped vegetables with the lemon juice and oil, and salt and pepper to taste.

Shake the hot potatoes so they split a little. Dress them with the sauce and the roasted cumin seeds, if used.

Serve hot, either on individual saucers or a single plate, with a fork for each guest.

Spinach or chard leaves dressed with vinegar
Espinacas o acelgas con vinagre

I had this delicious little dish in a *venta* (small country bar) in Baeza. It makes a very good first course for four if you double the quantities. Combine it with the recipe using chard stalks on page 76 if you are using chard.

makes 10 tapa mouthfuls / serves 2 as a starter

4 generous handfuls spinach or chard leaves
2 heaped tablespoons fresh breadcrumbs
4 tablespoons olive oil
1 tablespoon sherry vinegar
salt and pepper

Rinse, pick over, shred and wilt the leaves in a lidded pan with a little salt – allow 2-3 minutes. Drain thoroughly.

Meanwhile, fry the breadcrumbs golden in 2 tablespoons of the olive oil.

Toss the spinach with the remaining oil, the vinegar and freshly-ground pepper. Pile on a plate and top with the crisp breadcrumbs.

Green beans with spiced almonds
Judías verdes con almendras

This dish originates in Valencia, where five centuries ago the Moors planted almond groves for the preparation of chilled nut-milks and sherbets and to provide the raw material for their favourite honey and almond sweetmeats.

makes 12-15 tapa mouthfuls / serves 2 as a starter

2 generous handfuls green beans, trimmed and chopped
1-2 tablespoons flaked almonds
2-3 tablespoons olive oil
1 teaspoon hot pimentón
juice of ½ lemon
salt

Bring a pan of salted water to the boil, add the beans and cook them until tender but still green and firm – 3-4 minutes.

Meanwhile cut the flaked almonds into matchsticks. Heat the olive oil in a small frying pan (skillet) and fry the almonds golden – a few seconds only or you will burn both nuts and oil. Remove from the heat and stir in the pimentón.

Drain the beans and toss them with the lemon juice and the contents of the frying pan. Taste and adjust the seasoning.

Serve on a plate, with forks for each tapa eater.

Tomatoes stuffed with pine kernels
Tomates rellenos con piñones

Bite-sized tomatoes are perfect as tapas. For a first course for four, use large beef tomatoes and double the stuffing quantities.

makes 8 tapa mouthfuls / serves 2 as a starter
8 small tomatoes
3 tablespoons olive oil
1 tablespoon pine kernels or flaked almonds
1 tablespoon chopped onion
1 garlic clove, chopped
1 tablespoon chopped parsley
4 heaped tablespoons fresh breadcrumbs
salt and pepper

Preheat the oven to Gas Mark 7/220°C/425°F.

Wipe each tomato and slice off a small lid. Take out the seeds and discard them. Scoop out the centre flesh and reserve, along with the tomato lids.

Warm 2 tablespoons of the oil in a small pan and add the pine kernels or almond flakes. Let the nuts take colour, remove and drain. Add the onion and garlic to the pan juices and fry gently till soft and golden – 3-4 minutes. Tip in the reserved tomato flesh and allow the mixture to bubble up, mashing with a fork, to make a little sauce. Stir in the herbs, breadcrumbs and reserved nuts. Taste and add salt and pepper.

Arrange the hollow tomatoes in an oiled baking dish. Stuff them with the breadcrumb mix. Trickle with the rest of the oil and bake in the oven for 20-30 minutes until well-browned.

Serve the little tomatoes whole in their cooking dish, with forks or cocktail sticks for easy handling.

Peppers stuffed with rice and mushrooms
Pimientos rellenos con arroz y setas

This is – was – a speciality of the old Venta del Pilar just outside Alcoy in the hills behind Valencia. The dish was served hot in winter – it's cold in the shepherding uplands – and cool in summer.

makes 24-30 tapa mouthfuls / serves 4 as a starter
4 large red sweet or green peppers
2 tablespoons olive oil
2 garlic cloves, chopped
2-3 mushrooms, chopped
50 g/2 oz lean bacon or salt-cured ham, chopped
1 tablespoon mild pimentón
1 tablespoon chopped parsley
500 g/1 lb tomatoes, skinned and chopped
250 g/8 oz/1 cup paella rice
½ teaspoon salt
12 saffron threads infused in a little boiling water

Preheat the oven to Gas Mark 7/220°C/425°F.

Wipe the peppers and cut off a lid at the stalk end, leaving the stalk in place. Empty out the seeds.

Make a *sofrito*: heat the oil gently in a frying pan (skillet). Throw in the garlic and let it soften for a few moments. Add the mushrooms and bacon or ham and fry for a few more minutes. Stir in the pimentón, parsley, tomatoes and a wine glassful of water. Let the mixture bubble up. Stir in the rice, salt and saffron with its water, bubble up again and remove the pan from the heat.

Use the rice mixture to stuff the peppers – fill them only half full as the rice needs room to swell. In a baking dish, arrange the peppers upright, mouths pointing heavenwards and with their lids replaced.

Cover with foil and cook in the oven for about 1½ hours. Test after 1 hour by biting into a grain of rice from the top – it'll need to be very soft if the middle is properly tender.

Serve the peppers hot or cold, neatly cut into bite-sized portions in their cooking dish, with forks. If serving the peppers as a starter, allow one whole one for each person.

Courgettes (zucchini) in tomato sauce
Calabacines a la riojana

This is an aromatic vegetable stew from Don Quixote's home territory. Any vegetable – potatoes, beans, aubergines (eggplants), carrots – will respond happily to similar treatment.

makes 18-20 tapa mouthfuls / serves 3-4 as a starter
2-3 tablespoons olive oil
4-5 courgettes (zucchini), sliced into bite-sized rings
2 garlic cloves, chopped
1 medium-size onion, chopped
250 g/8 oz tomatoes, skinned and chopped (fresh or canned)
pinch thyme
1 bay leaf
1 wine glass of water
1 tablespoon chopped parsley
salt and pepper

Heat the olive oil in a saucepan. Throw in the courgettes (zucchini) and fry them for 2-3 minutes. Remove and reserve. Add the garlic

and onion to the pan and let them fry gently until they soften but do not take colour.

Add the chopped tomatoes, thyme and bay leaf; bubble up, mash lightly and let all simmer for a minute or two to a thick purée.

Return the courgettes (zucchini) to the pan. Pour in the water and bring all to the boil. Turn down the heat, lid and leave to simmer for 6-8 minutes, until the courgettes (zucchini) are tender but still bright green. If the sauce is too sloppy, boil it up fiercely for a moment or two. Taste and add salt and pepper. Stir in the parsley.

This dish is just as good hot or cold. Serve it in a shallow earth-brown earthenware casserole.

Vegetables with oil-and-garlic
Hervido con all-i-oli

Oil-and-garlic, Valencia's favourite dipping-sauce, is the traditional accompaniment to her beautiful vegetables, product of her fertile hinterline. In spring and early summer, the first of the crop are eaten raw.

makes 20-24 tapa mouthfuls / serves 3-4 as a starter
1 large carrot, scraped and cut into bite-sized lengths
1 large potato, peeled and cubed
1 turnip, peeled and cubed
½ cauliflower, divided into florets
a handful of green beans, topped and tailed
salt
garlic sauce
3-4 fresh, juicy garlic cloves
½ teaspoon salt
about 150 ml/ ¼ pint/ ⅔ cup olive oil

Bring a pan of salted water to the boil. If you have a good home-made stock – maybe from boiled beef, bacon or chicken – use that instead. Add the vegetables to the boiling liquid in the order listed,

bringing it back to the boil each time. The operation will take about 20 minutes.

While the vegetables cook, settle down with a pestle and mortar to make the sauce – a soothing process.

Chop the garlic roughly and crush it in the mortar with the salt. When the garlic is well pounded, start adding the oil in a thin stream. Keep pounding with the pestle and trickling in the oil until the mixture is good and thick.

Serve in its mortar or a small bowl, alongside the boiled vegetables for dipping.

Note: You can if you wish, work in an egg yolk for a thicker and richer but less piquant mix; or, if you are in a hurry, use a food processor or liquidiser, adding a slice of boiled potato, or a crust of well-moistened stale bread to stabilise the emulsion.

Whole broad bean casserole
Habas a la rondeña

This slow-cooked stew, aromatic with wine and herbs, is my favourite vegetable dish. I first tasted it in its home territory, the fortified hill-town of Ronda. The evening air is always cool in these mountains, even in summer, and many of the local dishes were traditionally simmered over a shallow brazier which used to do duty as central heating under the table. Double the quantities and finish with quarters of hard-boiled eggs for a perfect light summer lunch.

makes 15-20 tapa mouthfuls / serves 2 as a starter

500 g/1 lb young broad beans in their pods
3 tablespoons olive oil
1 small onion, chopped
1 garlic clove, chopped
1 tablespoon diced serrano ham or lean bacon
1 small glass of dry sherry
1 tablespoon fresh breadcrumbs

1 tablespoon chopped parsley
salt and pepper

Top, tail and string the young beans in their pods, and chop into short lengths, more or less following the swell of each bean. Do not do this in advance as the beans are inclined to turn navy blue at the edges. Podded beans can be used without further attention.

Warm the oil in a casserole or heavy pan. Fry the onion and garlic for a moment without allowing them to take colour. Add the chopped bacon or ham, and then the beans.

Pour in the sherry and its own volume of water, add salt and pepper, and bring all to the boil. Cover and stew gently for 1-1½ hours (this can also be done in a gentle oven at Gas Mark 3/160°C/325°F.) Check intermittently and add more water if necessary. When the beans are tender, bubble up uncovered for a moment to evaporate excess liquid – the dish should be juicy but not soupy.

Stir in the breadcrumbs and the parsley. Reheat, taste and add more salt and pepper if necessary.

Serve either in tapa portions in saucers, or in a pretty earthenware dish for sharing. Accompany with chunks of good bread to mop up the juices.

EGGS AND TORTILLAS

Eggs are the staple of the Spanish larder – as befits a rural economy with a strong peasant-farming tradition. The egg-lady, the *recovrera*, still, in the 1970's, collected surplus eggs from our neighbours in the remote Andalucían valley in which we lived. She would take the eggs to sell in the local market in Algeciras. Her suppliers would receive their payment in kind: salt and sugar, condensed milk and coffee – all items which could not be home-grown or made.

Any Spanish housewife who can wield more than a can-opener turns out a perfect Spanish omelette, the *tortilla española*. This is a thick, juicy egg-and-potato cake which bears only a passing resemblance to its frothy French cousin. There is a wide repertoire of these egg-cakes with many regional variations – visitors to Valencia will find a tapa bar serving nothing but different varieties of tortilla, dozens of them.

Eggs can be cooked either on an oil-rubbed griddle (*plancha*), or fried in shallow oil (*frito*), or cooked in a little oil in a shallow earthenware dish (*cazuela*) set over direct heat and served in the cooking dish (*al plato*). Alternatives are hard-boiled to eat with mayonnaise, or for inclusion in salads, or chopped and added to a stew or soup to compensate for a shortage of meat, or scrambled with diced chorizo or serrano ham or without vegetables cooked in olive oil – peppers, tomatoes, onions – as for the Basque *piparrada*.

Opposite: Spanish potato omelette

Spanish potato omelette
Tortilla española

The potato tortilla is not only the mainstay of the tapa table, it is staple picnic-fare all over Spain, and the nearest thing to a national dish. Children take it to school for lunch; grannies thrive on it; every household has its own special way of making it, the person who makes it best, and the perfect pan to cook it in. Garlic and parsley are sometimes included, but I like the clean fresh flavour of this simple recipe.

makes 20-24 bite-sized cubes / serves 4 as a starter
3 large free-range eggs
About 750 g/1½ lb potatoes (allow 1 medium
potato per large egg)
enough olive oil for shallow frying
(optional) 1 tablespoon finely chopped or slivered onion
salt

Peel and cut the potatoes into thin slices or chop into small dice or fat little fingers. Heat the oil in whatever you use to prepare a 2 person omelette. When a faint blue haze rises, add the potato, sprinkle with a little salt, and cook gently until quite soft but not yet browned, adding the onion half way through so that it softens but doesn't take colour.

Transfer the potato and onion to a sieve placed over a bowl to catch the oil as it drains and leave to cool a little.

Fork the eggs to blend and stir in the potato-onion. Pour most of the oil out of the pan, leaving only a tablespoon or two. Return the pan to the heat and tip in the egg mixture. The heat should be low or the base will burn before the eggs are ready. With a metal spatula, push the potato down into the egg so that all is submerged, lifting the set base to allow the raw egg to begin to set and neatening the sides to produce a deep straight edge. Pop a lid on top to reflect the heat back into the pan, and leave to set gently – allow 6-7 minutes.

As soon as the top begins to set, slide the tortilla out on to a plate; then invert it back into the pan to cook the other side. A little more oil in the pan may be necessary. Don't overcook the tortilla – the centre should remain juicy – allow another couple of minutes. When the under-surface is lightly gilded, slip the tortilla onto a plate and pat away excess oil with kitchen paper.

Serve the tortilla at room temperature, cut into bite-sized squares, each pierced with a cocktail stick (see photo page 93).

Sacro-Monte omelette
Tortilla al Sacromonte

Granada's celebrated tortilla is – or was – a speciality of the gypsy-quarter, a community of cave-dwellers which established itself in the cliffs above the Alhambra in the days of the Moors. The presence of variety meats, assorted bits and pieces of offal the butcher couldn't sell to the city's wealthy burgers, makes it a dish of the urban poor. The rich were missing a treat.

makes 20-24 bite-sized cubes / serves 2 as a main course

1 lamb's brains
2-3 lamb sweetbreads
3-4 tablespoons olive oil
1 large potato, peeled and cubed small (optional)
2 lamb's kidneys, skinned, cored and sliced thinly
2 tablespoons diced serrano ham or lean bacon
1 tablespoon diced red pepper
2 tablespoons shelled peas or broad beans
4 medium eggs
salt and pepper

Simmer the brain and sweetbreads in enough lightly salted water to cover. When they are firm and cooked through – about 20 minutes – drain and leave to cool, weighted between two plates to allow them to firm. Skin and dice.

Meanwhile heat the oil in a small omelette pan. Add the potato cubes (if you have plenty of brains and sweetbreads, the potato can be omitted). Cook the potato until just soft – don't let the temperature rise enough to brown it – and transfer to a sieve over a bowl to catch the drippings.

Fry the diced variety meats till they take a little colour. Transfer to the sieve with potato. Fry the kidneys with the ham or bacon and transfer to the sieve. Last of all, cook the peas or beans in the pan-drippings with a little water – a minute or two, just enough to warm them through.

Fork the eggs with salt and pepper and stir in the contents of the sieve.

Return the oil drippings from the bowl to the pan and reheat. Tip in the egg mixture, and cook it as in the previous recipe, forming it into a thick pancake and turning it once to set both sides. Keep the heat low at all times. Serve warm or cool, cut into bite-sized cubes and speared with cocktail sticks.

Countrywoman's omelette
Tortilla a la payesa

This is a fine solid omelette, a meal in itself, and excellent for a winter picnic. The recipe appears throughout the peninsula, made with regional varieties of cured sausage and whatever vegetables are in season.

makes 20-24 bite-sized cubes / serves 2 as a main course
4–5 tablespoons olive oil
1 large potato, peeled and diced
1 tablespoon diced serrano ham or lean bacon
1 garlic clove, slivered
1 tablespoon diced onion
1 ripe tomato, de-seeded and diced
handful green beans, diced
4 tablespoons shelled peas (fresh or frozen)
4 medium eggs
salt and pepper

Heat half oil in an omelette pan. Add the diced potato, salt lightly, lid loosely and cook gently until tender. Remove and drain in a sieve set over a bowl to catch the drippings.

Reheat the oil and fry the ham or bacon with the garlic and onion gently until the onion is soft. Add the tomato, green beans and peas or broad beans and bubble up till the tomato collapses into a little sauce.

Fork the eggs with salt and pepper to blend, and fold in the reserved diced potato and the contents of the pan.

Wipe out the pan, add the rest of the oil and the drippings from the bowl, and reheat. Tip in the egg mixture and cook as a thick pancake, neatening the sides and turning it once, as for the potato omelette.

Serve warm or at room temperature cut into neat bite-sized cubes and speared with cocktail sticks.

Beans and sausage omelette
Tortilla catalana

This is a popular tapa omelette in the bars of Barcelona, capital of Cataluña. The sausage used is butifarra, the Catalan's version of the southerners' chorizo. Butifarra is spiced with cinnamon, cloves and nutmeg, as befits a city-port which handled the spice trade.

makes 15-20 bite-sized cubes / serves 2 as a main course
2 tablespoons olive oil
2 tablespoons cubed butifarra or chorizo plus 1 teaspoon mixed spice
250 g/8 oz pre-cooked white beans or chickpeas
3 large eggs
salt and pepper

Warm a tablespoon of the olive oil in an omelette pan. Fry the sausage for a few minutes until the edges brown and the fat begins to run. Stir in the spices if using chorizo. Add the beans and bubble up to warm them through and blend the flavours. Leave to cool a little.

Fork the eggs lightly with salt and pepper and fold in the contents of the pan.

Wipe the pan and then heat the rest of the oil. Tip in the egg mixture and cook gently, loosely lidded, neatening the sides and turning it once, as for the potato tortilla.

Serve warm or cool, cut into neat bite-sized cubes and speared with cocktail sticks.

Spinach omelette
Tortilla de espinacas

This Valencian tortilla makes an excellent fresh-flavoured tapa. It's one of my own favourites for a light summer lunch.

makes 12-15 bite-sized cubes / serves 2 as a main course
4 generous handfuls spinach
1 tablespoon toasted pine kernels
4 eggs
2 tablespoons olive oil
salt and pepper

Wash the spinach and pick over the leaves, discarding any tough stalks. Pack into a roomy pan and cook briefly over a high heat in the water which clings to the leaves after washing. Drain as soon as the leaves wilt, tip into a sieve and press dry. Squeeze out any remaining water, and chop.

Fork the eggs with salt and pepper to blend. Stir in the spinach and toasted pine kernels.

Heat the oil in a small omelette pan. Tip in the egg mixture. Cook as a thick pancake, as for the potato omelette, turning it once and neatening the sides with a spatula to keep a firm edge.

Serve warm or cool, cut into bite-sized cubes and speared with cocktail sticks.

Omelette in spiced parsley sauce
Tortilla en salsa de Clavijo

This unusual tortilla – an oddity in that it includes Old World bread-crumbs rather the New World's potato and that you can make it ahead and reheat it in its sauce – is a speciality of Clavijo near Logroño. The use of Moorish spicing reflects centuries of life under the Muslims and Clavijo itself is the site of a battle in which St James, patron saint of the Christian kings of northern Spain, miraculously intervened to deliver a famous victory against the Muslims of An-dalucía, earning the warrior saint his sobriquet, Matamoros, – Moor-slayer.

makes 16-20 bite-sized cubes / serves 4 as a starter

4 heaped tablespoons fresh white breadcrumbs
4 tablespoons creamy milk
4 medium eggs
2-3 tablespoons olive oil
salt and pepper

for the sauce
2 tablespoons olive oil
1 tablespoon plain (all-purpose) flour
¼ teaspoon ground cloves
½ teaspoon ground cinnamon
200 ml/7 fl oz/¾ cup milk or chicken stock
1 tablespoon chopped parsley
salt and pepper

Put the breadcrumbs to soak in the milk for about 10 minutes.

Fork the eggs to blend, mix in the breadcrumbs and season with salt and pepper.

Heat the oil in a small omelette pan – it should be good and hot. Pour in the egg mixture and pull the sides to the middle to allow the runny egg to feel the heat. Lid loosely and cook gently until the egg is set, neatening the sides with a palate knife. Slide the tortilla out on to a plate as soon as the top no longer looks wet, reheat the pan and add extra oil if necessary. Reverse the tortilla back into the pan and cook the other side. Remove and cut, when cool, into bite-sized squares.

Meanwhile make the sauce. Warm the oil in a small saucepan. Sprinkle in the flour and cook until sandy – don't let it brown. Add the spices and then whisk in the milk or stock. Bring to the boil and then simmer gently, whisking as it thickens. Stir in the parsley. Taste and add salt and pepper.

Reheat the tortilla pieces in the sauce. Serve hot, speared with cocktail sticks.

Artichoke omelette
Tortilla de alcachofas

The artichoke, a many-branched member of the thistle family, grows in its ancestral form all over Spain, making this a very venerable dish indeed.

makes 15-20 bite-sized cubes / serves 2 as a main course
4-5 medium-size artichokes
½ lemon
4-5 tablespoons olive oil
1 tablespoon diced serrano ham or lean bacon
4 medium eggs
salt and pepper

First prepare the artichokes – you need only the hearts. Remove the hard outside leaves and cut the stalk close to the base. Trim off the dark green tips of the leaves with a sharp knife, leaving only as much as is tender and pale. Scoop out the central inner leaves, nick out and discard the hairy choke, exposing the heart. Drop the heart into a bowl of cold water into which you have squeezed half a lemon. Continue till all the hearts are prepared.

When you're ready to cook, drain the artichoke hearts and slice thinly.

Warm the oil in a 2-person omelette pan and fry the slices gently until soft and just beginning to gild. Add the diced ham or bacon and transfer the contents of the pan to a sieve set over a small basin to catch the drippings. Leave to cool a little.

Fork the eggs together with salt and pepper and fold in the cooked artichokes and ham.

Return the drippings to the pan (you may need a little more oil), reheat and pour in the egg mixture. Cook as a thick pancake, as for the potato tortilla.

Serve warm or cool, cut into bite-sized cubes and speared with cocktail sticks.

Asparagus sprue omelette
Tortilla de espárragos trigueras

This is a favourite springtime tapa throughout Andalucía, where gypsies sell small bundles of wild asparagus in the markets. Bitter and sweet varieties are usually on offer, and the best mix is a few of the first and a lot of the second. The fine green stalks of cultivated asparagus – sprue – are perfect for this dish. Big fat white ones can be used – they should be trimmed and sliced very finely.

makes 15-20 bite-sized cubes / serves 3-4 as a starter
1 bundle – a hand-span – thin green asparagus
2-3 tablespoons olive oil
3 large eggs
salt and pepper

Snap off the hard woody ends of the asparagus and discard. Chop the rest of the stalks into pea-sized lengths.

Warm a tablespoon of the olive oil in an omelette pan. Turn the asparagus in the hot oil for a moment or two until it turns bright green and softens a little. Drain in a colander over a bowl for the oil drippings.

Beat the eggs lightly with salt and pepper and mix in the asparagus.

Reheat all the oil, including the drippings. Tip in the egg mixture and cook as for every other tortilla in this section – gently, loosely-lidded, neatening the sides with a spatula and turning the whole thing once to set the underside.

Serve warm or cool, cut into neat bite-sized cubes and speared with cocktail sticks.

Mushroom and garlic omelette
Tortilla de setas y ajos frescos

This is a popular summertime tapa in Valencia, where it is made with porcini or pine-forest fungi, saffron milkcaps (*lactaria deliciosa*) and fresh garlic. These last look like spring onions, are somewhat chewy and have a mild flavour since they are used before the cloves have had time to form. Wild garlic grows throughout Europe, and many countries, including Britain, have similar recipes. I give here a combination of garlic cloves and spring onions as a replacement for hard-to-find fresh garlic, and advise cultivated mushrooms, unless you have access to your own gathering-patch and can tell a parasol from a destroying angel.

makes 15-20 bite-sized cubes / serves 2 as a main course
375 g/12 oz button mushrooms
4 tablespoons olive oil
2 garlic cloves, sliced
2 large spring onions (white part only), sliced
4 eggs
salt and pepper

Wipe (don't rinse) and slice the mushrooms. Heat the oil in a small omelette pan. Add the mushrooms. Cook them gently until all their moisture has evaporated and the oil is clear again.

Remove and drain in a sieve over a bowl to catch the drippings.

Add the garlic and sliced spring onions to the remaining oil in the pan. Fry them gently until they soften. Add them to the mushrooms in the sieve.

Beat the eggs lightly with salt and pepper. Stir in the now-cooled vegetables.

Add the oil drippings to the oil in the pan. Reheat and tip in the egg mixture. Cook gently till just set, neatening the sides, lidding loosely and turning the whole thing once as soon as the top looks as if it's not too runny.

Serve warm or cool, cut into bite-sized cubes and speared with cocktail sticks.

Broad bean omelette
Tortilla de habas

The broad bean was the mainstay of the Spanish diet until Christopher Columbus brought back the haricot bean from the Americas. Spain's wide repertoire of bean-and-pork dishes were all originally based on the broad bean, which could be dried and stored. This recipe uses fresh beans; at the beginning of the season when the beans are young and tiny, use them whole – the pods have a delicate asparagus-like flavour – later in the year, slip them out of their leathery skins.

makes 15-20 bite-sized cubes /
serves 2 as a main course

2 tablespoons olive oil
4 heaped tablespoons tender young broad beans
1 tablespoon fresh mint leaves, shredded
½ wine glass of sherry
4 medium eggs
salt and pepper

Warm a tablespoon of the olive oil in an omelette pan. Add the beans, mint and sherry and bubble up to evaporate the alcohol. Add a splash of water, bubble up again, lid loosely and leave the beans to simmer gently for 10-15 minutes, until perfectly tender. Bubble up at the end to evaporate extra moisture, then leave aside to cool a little.

Fork the eggs with salt and pepper and mix in the contents of the pan.

Heat the rest of the oil in the omelette pan. Tip in the egg mixture and cook as a thick pancake, neatening the sides as it cooks, lidding loosely and turning the whole thing once to set the other side.

Serve warm or cool, cut into neat bite-sized cubes and speared with cocktail sticks.

Scrambled eggs with bacon and spiced sausage
Duelos y quebrantos

This dish of eggs scrambled with ham and spicy chorizo was Don Quixote's treat on a Saturday night. The name literally means wounds-and-suffering – perhaps because the paprika from the sausage bleeds into the eggs. It remains a standard dish in La Mancha, and makes a delicious little hot tapa.

makes 8-10 tapa mouthfuls / serves 2 as a starter

2 tablespoons diced salt-cured ham or lean bacon
2 tablespoons diced chorizo, or salami with
½ teaspoon paprika
1 tablespoon olive oil
2 eggs
salt and pepper
squares of bread, to serve

Fry the ham or bacon and the diced sausage in the oil in a small frying pan (skillet). Cook until the meat browns a little and the fat runs. Stir in the paprika if you are using salami.

Meanwhile, lightly fork up the eggs with a little salt and pepper. Add the eggs to the contents of the pan. Turn up the heat. Turn the mixture so that the eggs scramble. As soon as they begin to set, remove the pan from the heat.

Serve on bite-sized squares of bread, each speared with a cocktail stick.

Scrambled eggs with summer vegetables
Piparrada

A deliciously juicy combination of eggs and vegetables, this Basque speciality is one of the world's great dishes, It makes a very fine tapa, or the quantities given will make a light lunch for two. The vegetables can be prepared ahead, and the eggs scrambled in at the last minute. Aubergines (eggplants) and courgettes (zucchini) are sometimes among the diced vegetables used.

makes 12-15 tapa mouthfuls / serves 4 as a starter
2 tablespoons olive oil
1 garlic clove, chopped finely
2 tablespoons finely chopped onion
2 tablespoons chopped green pepper
2 tablespoons chopped red pepper
1 large ripe tomato, de-seeded and diced
2 medium eggs, forked to blend
12-15 small squares of bread, fried in olive oil
salt and pepper

Heat the oil in a roomy frying pan (skillet). Turn the garlic, onion and peppers in the hot oil until they soften and take a little colour. Add the tomato and bubble up to make a jammy little sauce.

Stir in the egg and stir till lightly set. Season with salt and pepper and spoon onto squares of fried bread. Serve speared with cocktail sticks.

Mixed vegetable omelette
Tortilla murciana

This is a delicious omelette from the fertile market gardens of Murcia, a handsome city founded by the Moors. Any combination of vegetables will work – just make sure the proportion of vegetable to egg remains roughly equal (pretty much the rule with all tortillas).

makes 20-24 bite-sized cubes / serves 2 as a main course
4-5 tablespoons olive oil
1-2 carrots, diced small
generous handful green beans, trimmed and diced
1-2 smallish courgettes (zucchini), sliced thinly
4 tablespoons shelled peas or broad beans (fava)
1 tablespoon diced serrano ham or lean bacon
1 garlic clove, chopped
1 green pepper, de-seeded and diced
3 medium eggs
salt and pepper

Heat 3 tablespoons of the oil in an omelette pan. Add the carrots, beans, courgettes (zucchini) and peas or broad beans in the order given, turning them in the hot oil with a splash of water for 3-4 minutes, till the water has evaporated and the vegetables are just tender. Remove and drain in a sieve over a bowl to catch the drippings.

Reheat the pan with the rest of the oil and add the ham or bacon, garlic and diced green pepper. Fry gently for 2-3 minutes. Remove and drain with the other vegetables.

Beat the eggs lightly with salt and pepper. Stir in the cooked ingredients.

Return the drippings to the pan and reheat. Tip in the egg mixture and cook gently till the mixture forms a firm pancake with a soft heart, neatening the sides, lidding loosely and turning the tortilla once – slide it out onto a plate and reverse it back into the pan – to cook the underside.

Serve warm or cool, cut into bite-sized cubes and speared with cocktail sticks.

Griddle-cooked quail's eggs
Huevos de codorniz a la plancha

Happily for the population of small wild birds, quail-farming has recently caught on in Spain. I first had these eggs fried on a hot griddle (Spanish cookers have one automatically built in) in a tapa bar in a village in the hills behind Ronda. The little eggs make perfect bite-sized tapas – they are much smaller than hen's eggs, and keep their shape when cooked.

makes 6 tapa mouthfuls / serves 2-3 as a starter

6 quail's eggs
1 tablespoon olive oil
6 small round slices of fresh bread or toast
salt and pepper

Fry the eggs on a very hot griddle or heavy frying pan (skillet) slicked with the olive oil.

Slip each egg on to its round of bread or toast and sprinkle with salt and pepper. That's all. Miniature perfection!

FISH, PRAWNS, SHRIMPS AND SHELLFISH

Spain harvests magnificent seafood from its surrounding coasts. Most of this bounty from both Atlantic and Mediterranean waters is marketed fresh and unprocessed, trucked through the night to ensure that the inland cities like Madrid get their fish as soon as possible after it is caught. So wide is the variety that the vocabulary to describe the different sea-creatures changes from coast to coast, and even from port to port. When choosing in a bar, the eye and the finger are often the only communication possible to all but the native-born. To make this easy, sea delicacies are usually laid out for the customers' inspection on a cold counter, priced by weight, and cooked fresh to order.

Prawns and the larger crustaceans are a luxury, with prices to match – which means they do not usually appear as a free tapa, but as an individually priced *ración* or portion. Less familiar sea-creatures include sea-tomatoes, sea-lemons, sea-dates, sea-urchins, spiky-shelled sea-snails, and a wide variety of shore-crabs. Most esteemed of all is the *percebe* or goose-necked barnacle, a lobster-fleshed sea-creature which looks like a bunch of miniature elephants' feet. Add to that a basketful of the more familiar bi-valves – mussels, oysters, clams, razor-shells, scallops, cockles – and it is easy to see why so many Spanish tapa bars specialise in seafood.

The housewives of Andalucía have the lightest hand with the fish-

Opposite: Griddled Tuna Steaks

fryer in all Spain. There's nothing which can be trawled or netted or gathered from the shore-line which can't be frittered and fried – dusted through the rough bread-flour milled from the sun-ripened wheat grown on the floodplain of the Guadalquivir, and dropped into a shallow pool of lightly smoking olive oil. The catch ranges from sea-anemones to the pin-head-small *chunquetes* (now forbidden fruit); from the tiny jumping shrimps of Cádiz, to steaks cut from the great tuna caught on migration through the Straits of Gibraltar.

Griddled tuna or swordfish steaks
Atún o pez espada a la plancha

Both swordfish and fresh tuna are popular in Spain. They are widely available inland, since their great size makes them ideal for transportation. They are treated more like steak than fish, and are often served as the main course in a meal.

makes 16 tapa mouthfuls / serves 4 as a starter

8 thin-cut tuna or swordfish steaks
1 tablespoon olive oil
2-3 cos lettuce leaves, shredded
salt and pepper
quartered lemon, to serve

Put the fish to soak for 30 minutes in cold salted water to drain out any blood. Drain and pat dry. Rub the cut surfaces with the oil and sprinkle with salt and pepper.

Heat a griddle or heavy iron frying pan (skillet) until it is smoking hot. Smack on the steaks. Griddle them fast for 2-3 minutes a side, turning once.

Divide into bite-sized pieces, and spear each piece with a cocktail stick on a small bit of the lettuce leaf. Serve with lemon quarters. (see photo page 111)

Fried fish
Pescado frito

Each port has its own preferred mixture of fish for frying. Bargains are not easy to come by, though the tail piece of any large fish which has been cut into steaks can fit the bill, as indeed can the tidbits from the head. Of this last, hake cheeks and throats are particularly prized for tapa portions. The cheeks can be fried, but the throats should be cooked on their own in a hot dry pan or earthenware casserole – a few moments' shaking the little morsels over the heat produces a creamy little sauce.

makes 15-20 tapa mouthfuls / serves 2 as a starter
250 g/8 oz fish fillets or cutlets, skinned and boned
2-3 tablespoons milk or water
3-4 tablespoons seasoned coarse plain (all-purpose) flour
(mix in a little fine semolina for a really crisp coating)
oil for shallow-frying (half olive, half sunflower is perfect)
salt
lemon or bitter orange quarters, to serve

Trim the fish into neat bite-sized pieces: fillets can be cut into strips: slice across the diagonal for extra strength – the cross-grain holds the flesh together.

Dip the prepared fish first in milk or water and then dust through the seasoned flour, shaking off any excess.

Heat a thumb's-width of oil in a small frying pan (skillet). When the surface is lightly hazed with blue, slip in the fish pieces – not too many at a time so that the temperature of the oil remains high. Fry the fish briefly – just long enough to firm the flesh and gild the covering – turning each piece once. Remove with care and drain on kitchen paper.

Sprinkle with salt, spear each morsel with a cocktail stick and serve with quarters of lemon or bitter orange.

Breadcrumbed marinated fish
Pescado en adobo rebozado

This recipe comes from a bar in the old Jewish quarter of Seville; the bar's main house-speciality is Manchego cheese matured in olive oil.

The marination in lemon and garlic adds a Mediterranean flavour to plain white fish.

makes 16 tapa mouthfuls /
serves 2 as a light main course

8 thin-cut firm white fish steaks weighing about 25-50 g/1-2 oz each (swordfish, monkfish, tuna, hake)
juice of 1 lemon
1 garlic clove, chopped
1 egg, beaten with 1 tablespoon milk
3-4 tablespoons fine toasted breadcrumbs
oil for frying (olive and sunflower is a good mix)
salt and pepper

Put the fish steaks to marinate for an hour or two in the lemon juice, garlic and salt and pepper. Remove, drain well and dip first in the beaten egg, then press firmly into the breadcrumbs to give the pieces a little jacket.

Heat the oil until it is lightly hazed with blue. Slip in the steaks 2 to 3 at a time so that the oil temperature does not cool too much. Turn them once, remove and drain on kitchen paper.

Serve hot, with cocktail sticks for easy handling.

Pickled sardines
Escabeche de sardinas

This recipe is very popular in Roquetas del Mar on the coast of Almería. The pickle originally served to conserve the sardine catch in the days before refrigeration. It remains a popular dish today. The pickled fish will keep for a week in the fridge.

makes 12-15 tapa portions / serves 4 as a starter
500 g/1 lb fresh sardines or small herring
2 garlic cloves, sliced
1 bay leaf, crumbled
1 wine glass white wine vinegar
2 tablespoons olive oil
salt and pepper

Preheat the oven to Gas Mark 3/160°C/325°F.

If your fishmonger hasn't already done so, prepare the fish: rub off the scales under running water and remove the guts by slitting the bellies with a knife and pulling out the innards. Trim off the heads and layer half the fish neatly into a baking dish or earthenware cazuela, sprinkle with garlic, bay leaf and salt and pepper and top with the rest of the fish. Bring the vinegar and the same volume of water to the boil and then pour it round the fish. Trickle with the oil and cover with foil.

Bake in the oven for half an hour. Leave to cool. Serve warm or at room temperature. Depending on the size of the fish, cut into bite-sized pieces and spear each with a cocktail stick.

Fried anchovies
Boquerones fritos

The freshness of the fish – along with the quality of flour, salt and olive oil combined with the skill of the cook – all contribute to the success of this simple dish. Anchovies, shoal-fish which once appeared in vast numbers in the inshore fishing grounds of the Mediterranean, are still numerous enough to be sold cheap wherever they're landed, making them the most popular tapa in the seaside bars of Cadiz and Malaga.

makes 8-10 tapa mouthfuls / serves 2 as a starter
500 g/1 lb fresh anchovies
2-3 heaped tablespoons plain (all-purpose) flour

sea salt
oil for frying (a mixture of olive and sunflower is good)
lemon quarters, to serve

Gut the little fish – you can do this just by running your finger down the soft belly, or by slitting the belly with a sharp knife and pulling out the innards. (Sardines will need scaling first.) Behead them or not as you please. Rinse, drain and dry the fish.

Sieve the flour and salt on to a plate. Pinch the tails of the fish together in fans of 3 to 5, depending on size. Dust the little fans through the flour, making sure the tails are firmly stuck together.

Heat enough oil to submerge the little fans in a shallow frying pan or skillet. When the surface is lightly hazed with blue, slip in the fish fans head first, adding only 2 or 3 bunches at a time. Fry till crisp and golden, turning them once. Transfer to kitchen paper to drain. Continue till all are done.

Serve the crisp little fish piping hot, one fan per tapa, accompanied by a lemon quarter.

Grilled (broiled) sardines
Sardinas asadas

This is the most popular way of preparing the fine fat sardines trawled by the inshore fleet. Fresh-caught sardine flash a brilliant rainbow of colour – green, turquoise and scarlet on silver flanks. Don't de-scale the fish for grilling (broiling) – the scales and the natural oil in the skin prevent them sticking.

makes 8-9 tapa portions / serves 2-3 as a starter
500 g/1 lb perfectly fresh sardines
sea salt
lemon quarters, to serve

Rinse and gut the fish. Gutting is easily done with your index finger through the belly; for larger fish, slit the belly with a knife and pull

out the innards from the head downwards. Leave the heads and tails in place if small, remove the heads of larger, and sprinkle the skin with salt.

Heat the grill or barbecue until the metal is really hot. Place on the fish and let them take the heat, turning them once, until the skin blisters black and bubbly. The thicker the fish the longer they will need – 3-4 minutes a side should be ample for even the largest fish.

Serve one fish per tapa (two if small) and use your fingers – etiquette dictates you work from head to tail, nibbling first one side and then the other. Lemon quarters and bread serve for wiping fishy fingers.

Monkfish kebabs
Pinchitos de rape

These rather Moorish kebabs were a speciality of a now-vanished beach bar in Torremolinos back in the days when this popular seaside resort was nothing more than a fishing village. Swordfish can be used instead of the monkfish. Moorish skewers are very thin raw iron, with steel knitting needles the alternative in the days when anyone knitted their own. Bamboo skewers are a good alternative – don't forget to soak them or they'll burst into flame.

makes 12-15 tapa mouthfuls / serves 2 as a starter
350 g/12 oz filleted monkfish
1 large green pepper
2 tablespoons olive oil
1 lemon, juice and grated zest
1-2 garlic cloves, crushed
1 teaspoon cumin seeds
salt and pepper
cubes of bread, to serve

Cut the fish fillets into bite-sized cubes. Hull, de-seed and cut the green pepper into matching squares. Thread the monkfish alternating with the green peppers on long fine skewers and arrange on a plate.

Prepare an aromatic marinade by combining the oil, lemon juice and zest with the crushed garlic, cumin, salt and pepper, and pour it over the skewered fish. Cover with clingfilm and leave in a cool place for an hour or two to take the flavours.

Remove the fish-skewers from the marinade and shake or pat to get rid of excess moisture.

Heat a griddle or grill to maximum heat. Grill (broil) the skewers fiercely for a couple of minutes on each side – just till the fish flesh turns opaque and the pepper pieces caramelise a little.

Serve with a cube of bread speared on the end of each skewer.

Spiced mackerel
Caballa en escabeche

When a fishing fleet finds a shoal of mackerel, it catches them by the boatful. In pre-refrigeration days, spiced pickle-baths were a way not only to conserve the catch for a few extra days, but also to add variety to the diet. Use this pickle to spice leftover cod or haddock in batter, or any leftover fried fish.

makes 12-14 tapa mouthfuls / serves 3-4 as a starter

500 g/1 lb mackerel (or fillets of cod or haddock)
1 heaped tablespoon plain (all-purpose) flour
2 tablespoons olive oil
1 slice of onion
1 garlic clove, sliced
1 small carrot, sliced
1 tablespoon chopped parsley
1 teaspoon oregano
1 bay leaf
4 black peppercorns, crushed
4 tablespoons sherry or wine vinegar
2 tablespoons water
¼ teaspoon cayenne pepper
salt

Gut the mackerel – slit the belly with a sharp knife and pull out the innards – then behead and wipe. Chop it straight across the bone to give 6 or 7 thick slices. Sprinkle the slices with salt and dust them with the flour.

Heat the oil in a shallow frying pan (skillet). When it is blue-hazed, put in the fish – don't let the oil overheat. Fry the cutlets golden (a few minutes only so that the fish remains firm); then transfer them to a wide shallow dish.

If you are using leftover fried fish, start the recipe here.
Fry the onion and garlic gently in the oil which remains in the pan (add a little more if you need it). Stir in the carrot, parsley, oregano, bay leaf and peppercorns. Allow the aromatics to fry gently for a few moments so that the flavours blend. Add the vinegar and water, stir in the cayenne and a little salt, and allow the mixture to bubble up. Scrape in all the bits that stick to the bottom of the pan. Pour this warm scented bath unstrained over the fish.

Cover loosely with a clean cloth, and leave at least overnight in a cool place. This is ready to eat in a day, better in two. Serve a bite-sized piece per tapa, speared with a cocktail stick.

Cuttlefish or squid in its own ink
Chipirones o calamares en su tinta

A Basque speciality, this delicious way of preparing inkfish is popular all over Spain. The cuttlefish is a squid-like creature, but rounder and darker in the body than squid. It has a porous white 'bone' (nature's toothpowder, much appreciated by canaries) instead of the squid's transparent stick. Cuttlefish and squid ink is splendidly black – a kind of oceanic soot which dyes everything it touches. It has a delicate flavour all its own which makes the effort of collecting it worthwhile (though if you prefer you can now buy small sachets of squid ink). The recipe is too time-consuming to be worth making in smaller quantities.

makes 20-24 tapa mouthfuls / serves 4 as a starter
500 g/1 lb small cuttlefish or squid
4 tablespoons olive oil
2 onions, chopped
2 garlic cloves, chopped
500 g/1 lb tomatoes, skinned and chopped (fresh or canned)
1 tablespoon fresh breadcrumbs
1 tablespoon chopped parsley
salt and pepper

Wash the cuttlefish or squid thoroughly – they're sandy creatures, even when small. Push your finger into the cap and take out the cuttle or the little plasticky 'bone', and pull the tentacles and innards delicately away from the body. Look for the silvery ink sacks among the innards. It doesn't matter if you can't find all the sacks – 1 or 2 is quite enough to turn the dish midnight black. Break the sacks into a small sieve placed over a bowl. Reserve the inky liquid.

Remove and discard the beaks, eyes and the soft innards of the fish. Chop the tentacles into small pieces and use them to stuff the hollow bodies.

Warm the oil in a deep-sided frying pan (skillet). Add the onions and garlic and fry gently until they soften. Add the tomatoes. Let the mixture bubble up and cook it down to a thickish sauce. Lay in the fish and reheat till just below bubbling, lid loosely and simmer gently for 8-10 minutes – any longer and fish flesh will harden – adding a little hot water as necessary so that the juices do not dry out. Transfer the fish to a warm plate while you finish the sauce.

Mash up the ink with the breadcrumbs and parsley and stir in the contents of the pan – you can sieve it if you like a smooth sauce, or drop it all in the liquidiser and process till smooth. The sauce will now be inky black. Heat it gently in the pan, season with salt and pepper, return the reserved fish to the sauce and reheat till almost bubbling.

To serve either cut the bodies into rings and fill each ring with some sauce or serve one fish and a dab of sauce per tapa, each speared with a cocktail stick.

Baked scallops
Vieiras de Santiago de Compostela

The scallop or pilgrim-shell, unlike most of its fellow bi-valves, is a wanderer, propelling itself backwards through the world's oceans in its perpetual search for food. In recognition of this, scallop shells were worn by medieval pilgrims in their hats to indicate that they were on their way to the great shrine of Santiago de Compostela. Because of this, the scallop is a recurrent decorative motif all along Europe's pilgrim routes.

makes 6 tapa portions / serves 3 as a starter

6 scallops (live in shells, if possible)
3-4 tablespoons olive oil
1 teaspoon plain (all-purpose) flour
1 garlic clove, finely slivered
2 tablespoons finely-chopped onion
1 heaped tablespoon chopped parsley
1 wine glassful dry sherry or white wine
2 tablespoons grated cheese
salt and pepper

Rinse the scallops, discarding the sandy little digestive tract and the eye-frill, and slice horizontally into 2-3 discs, leaving the corals whole and reserving the curved sides of the shells (if available).

Heat a tablespoon of the oil in a heavy frying pan (skillet). Lay in the scallop meat (reserving the delicate corals) and cook briefly in the hot oil until the surfaces caramelise a little – allow no more than a minute per side. Remove and reserve.

Reheat the juices in the pan with another tablespoon of oil, add the garlic and onion and fry gently till soft (no hurry – don't let the vegetables take colour). Sprinkle in the flour and add the sherry or wine. Bubble up to evaporate the alcohol, add half a glass of water and stir, scraping in any sticky bits from the pan, and bubble up again to make a little sauce. Stir in the parsley and season with salt and pepper and maybe a little sugar to cut the acidity of the wine. Slip the corals into the hot sauce, allow them to poach for a minute or two, then return the reserved scallop disks to the pan. Spoon all back into the shells or divide between six little individual cazuelas (earthenware baking dishes).

Sprinkle with the grated cheese and the remaining trickle of oil. Finish under the grill until gilded and bubbling.

Grilled (broiled) prawns
Gambas a la parilla

Prawns for grilling (broiling) should be raw when you start. Ready-cooked ones are at their best served cold with mayonnaise (page 38) and/or chopped vegetable sauce (page 46).

makes 7-8 tapa portions / serves 2 as a starter
250 g/8 oz large raw prawns (fresh or frozen)
1 tablespoon olive oil
1 tablespoon salt
1 lemon, quartered, to serve

Rub the whole prawns, unpeeled and with the heads left on, with a slick of oil. Salt them heavily – plenty of salt on the skin enhances the natural sweetness of the flesh inside.

Heat the grill or barbecue until it is sizzling hot. Slap on the prawns. Let them cook, turning once – 2-3 minutes on each side should be enough. Serve with quartered lemon and bread for wiping fishy fingers.

Grilled (broiled) oysters
Ostras gratinadas

If you are catering for those who like their oysters raw, do not interfere with their pleasure. Otherwise this is a deliciously simple way of preparing the king of shellfish.

makes 6 tapa portions / serves 1-2 as a starter
6 oysters
2-3 tablespoons fresh breadcrumbs
1 tablespoon chopped parsley, to serve

Carefully open the oysters by levering apart with a knife. Leave them on their deep half-shell.

Sprinkle each oyster with a little hat of breadcrumbs, parsley and garlic. Finish with a trickle of oil. Pop the oysters under the grill until they plump up and sizzle.

Serve one oyster per person, with a lemon quarter on the side.

Fried squid
Calamares fritos

Squid and cuttlefish, from the hefty *calamar* to the tiny *chipirón*, are perfect material for the fryer. Very small cuttlefish can be cooked whole – they are delicious but must be very fresh, and – be warned – they're sure to spit oily juices all over the stove. More widely available are the larger squid (they grow up to two feet long), whose milk-white bodies can be cut into neat rings. To prepare any of the smaller cephalopods (squid, small octopus, cuttlefish) straight from the net, see instructions on p.122.

makes 12-15 tapa mouthfuls / serves 2 as a starter
250 g/8 oz prepared squid, cut into rings and
short lengths of tentacle
3-4 tablespoons bread flour

1 large egg, forked to blend
oil for frying (half olive, half sunflower is perfect)
salt
lemon quarters, to serve

Rinse the squid and pat it dry.

Dust each ring through the flour; then dip it into the egg forked up with its own volume of water. Do not add salt at this stage: Spanish cooks do not salt squid, cuttlefish or octopus before cooking – salting, they say, toughens the flesh, and they should know: Spanish housewives handle a great deal of squid.

Heat the frying oil until you can see a faint blue haze rising from the surface. Test the heat with a cube of bread first – it should colour as soon as it is dropped in.

Fry the rings, not too many a time, in the hot oil. Drain and sprinkle with salt. Serve hot, with lemon quarters.

Clams in sherry
Almejas en vino de jerez

Shellfish are trucked all over Spain from as far away as the Scottish Hebrides – Spanish cooks like their shellfish alive on the shell and prepare them in simple recipes which make the most of their delicate flavour. This is the classic way to prepare any bi-valve using the native-grown wine of Andalucía.

makes 12 tapa portions / serves 2-3 as a starter
500 g/1 lb small clams or mussels in their shells
1 tablespoon olive oil
1 garlic clove, chopped
1 tablespoon chopped parsley
1 wine glass of dry sherry

Wash the shellfish in plenty of cold water, checking over and dis-

carding any which are broken or that don't close when handled. Leave to soak in cold water for an hour or two.

Put the oil to heat in a wide shallow frying pan (skillet) (I use a wok). When the oil is lightly hazed with smoke, toss in the garlic and fry for a moment. Add the parsley and the wine. When it is good and hot, add the shellfish.

Cover with a lid and shake the pan over the heat so that all the shellfish have a chance to cook. If you have no lid, keep moving the shells with a draining-spoon. Allow 3-4 minutes for all the shells to open. Remove from the heat and pick out and discard any that remain closed. Serve hot or warm without delay. They should not be reheated or they will be rubbery. Leftovers make a good addition to a sea food salad.

Serve 2 or 3 in their shells as a tapa, sauced with a little of the aromatic juice.

Winkles or whelks with spiced vinegar
Bigarros o bocinas con vinagre

The winkle supplied early man with his tapas – periwinkle shells are found in prehistoric middens all over Europe. In Spain the most highly appreciated sea-mollusc is the spiky-shelled *canadilla*, murex, a Mediterranean sea-snail for which winkles and whelks can substitute – they conform to the spirit if not the letter of the delicacy.

makes 10-12 tapa portions / serves 3-4 as a starter
500 g/1 lb winkles or whelks
1 dried chilli, de-seeded
6 peppercorns, crushed
½ teaspoon crushed coriander seeds
1 bay leaf, torn into small pieces
small bottle of sherry vinegar
sea salt

If the shellfish is still raw, boil for 10-20 minutes in salted water, depending on size. Drain and rinse in cold water, and let them cool.

Meanwhile, put the aromatics into the bottle of vinegar and give it a good shake. The longer this is kept, the better it will be.

Serve the shellfish with pins or cocktail sticks and the spiced vinegar for dipping.

Grilled octopus dressed with olive oil and pimentón
Pulpo a la gallega

This is a speciality of the fishing communities of Galicia on Spain's rocky north-western coast. When the fleet is in port in winter, the dish is prepared with dried octopus, a popular store cupboard item all round the Mediterranean where it's sold as a leathery tangle of suckered arms.

makes 15-20 tapa mouthfuls / serves 2 as a starter
500 g/1 lb small octopus (or large cuttlefish or squid)
oil for brushing
the dressing
2 garlic cloves, chopped finely
1 tablespoon hot pimentón (smoked for preference)
6 tablespoons olive oil
salt

Wash the octopus thoroughly. If you are using squid or cuttlefish, prepare it according to the instructions on page 122. If you are dealing with octopus, bang the creature on a hard board to tenderise it first, bring a pan of unsalted water to the boil and dip the octopus in the boiling water three times to firm the flesh (this ritual is traditional – omit it if you dare).

Drain out the water and cook the octopus gently in its own liquid until tender – all the cephalopods can be cooked in their own juice, but keep checking just to be on the safe side and add a splash of boiling water if necessary. A small octopus takes about an hour, large squid and cuttlefish only about 30 minutes.

Meanwhile, make the dressing: pound the garlic to a mush with a little salt in a pestle with a mortar, then work in the pimentón and oil. Or whizz everything in the processor or liquidiser.

Drain the fish and pat dry. Preheat the grill or heavy iron griddle, brush the fish with a little oil and grill briefly on a high heat. Slice into bite-sized chunks and trickle with the dressing. Spike each chunk with a cocktail stick and accompany with bread to mop up the juices.

Fisherman's mussels
Mejillones a la marinera

Fresh mussels make the perfect tapa – they are cheap, exactly the right size for a mouthful, and come conveniently packaged in their own double-sided dish. They are very good cold, dressed with a little oil and a shellful of finely chopped onion, garlic, tomato and pepper. Cooked, they will keep for several days in the fridge. Any fresh live shellfish can replace the mussels.

makes 12-16 tapa mouthfuls / serves 2 as a starter
500 g/1 lb mussels in their shells (or cockles or clams)
1 tablespoon olive oil
1 garlic clove, chopped finely
1 tablespoon chopped parsley
1 wine glass of dry sherry
salt

Scrub the mussels and scrape off their little black beards (after this they won't survive for long). Discard any which feel unusually heavy (they're probably dead and full of sand) or do not close when handled.

Heat the oil in a wide pan (I use a wok). Throw in the garlic and

let it soften for a moment. Add the parsley and the sherry and salt.
Bubble it up and add the mussels. Lid, turn up the heat, and shake
till the shells open in the steam (if they don't open, discard).

That's all. Don't reheat: they're perfect as they are and are as good
cold as hot. Serve one or two shells per tapa.

Prawns in olive oil, garlic and chilli
Gambas al ajillo

This dish is one of the great pleasures of the tapa table. *Anguilas*,
baby eels (elvers), are also prepared *al ajillo* – with garlic – a method
also known as 'pil-pil' (the noise, you may be told, the cazuela
makes as it feels the heat of the flame). The prawns are served sizzling hot in their individual cooking dish, a small earthenware
cazuela, as a *ración* or single portion for sharing. Tapa bars which
specialise in these mouth-scalding preparations offer little wooden
forks so that customers do not burn their tongues. Crab is also excellent prepared in this way, though it'll need a splash of sherry or
brandy to keep it juicy.

makes 2-3 tapa portions / serves 1 as a starter
2 tablespoons olive oil
1 garlic clove, sliced
3-4 very small dried chillies
125 g/4 oz peeled raw prawns
salt

Heat the oil in an individual earthenware casserole, cazuela, set over
a high heat (or in the oven on maximum). When the oil is sizzling,
add the rest of the ingredients. Reheat for a minute or two to allow
the prawns to change colour in the hot oil.

Serve immediately in the cooking dish, with wooden forks or
cocktail sticks, and bread for mopping up the aromatic oil.

Crayfish with green sauce
Cigalas con salsa verde

This is a speciality of the Casa Antonio Marlin on the Malaga seafront beside the bullring. The green sauce is delicious with any cold fish or shellfish. It can be used to dress cold mussels or a seafood salad.

makes 8 tapa portions / serves 2 as a starter

8 raw crayfish or Dublin Bay prawns
salt

the sauce
4 tablespoons olive oil
1 tablespoon sherry- or wine vinegar or lemon juice
1 garlic clove, chopped finely
1 tablespoon finely chopped spring onion
1 tablespoon finely chopped parsley
sea salt

Bring a pan of well-salted water to the boil and throw in the raw crustaceans. Bring the water back to a rolling boil and allow 5 minutes cooking at a steady bubble. Remove the pan from the heat, lid and leave for another 5 minutes. Drain the fish and rinse through cold water to halt the cooking process.

Meanwhile mix the sauce ingredients together with a couple of tablespoons of water and leave to develop the flavours for an hour or so, while the crayfish cool and firm.

Serve the crayfish with their sauce.

Shrimp fritters
Tortillitas de camarones

These crisp little fritters are sold hot from the frying vat on street corners in the windswept port of Cádiz. They are made with tiny jumping-shrimps, *camarones*, caught by small boys in buckets in the long sandy shallows which edge the famous salt flats beyond the town. While chickpea flour is usual, you can use any of the Indian chappati flours or even a stone-ground wholemeal.

makes 10-12 small fritters / serves 2 as a starter

4 heaped tablespoons chickpea flour
½ teaspoon bicarbonate of soda
½ teaspoon salt
2 tablespoons olive oil
1 tablespoon grated onion
1 tablespoon chopped parsley
About 4 tablespoons whole tiny shrimps, unshelled
oil for frying

Sieve the flour, bicarbonate of soda and salt into a bowl, and gradually blend in the oil and enough water (about 8 tablespoons) to make a thin pouring batter. Stir in onion and parsley and fold in the shrimps.

Heat enough oil in a pan to just submerge the fritters. When it's hazed with blue, drop in the shrimp-laden batter by the tablespoonful – not too many at a time or the oil temperature will drop. Fry golden and crisp, turning once. Flatten the fritters with a draining spoon as they cook, to make sure the batter is well spread out so that they are crisp all the way through. Serve piping hot straight from the pan.

Clams in tomato sauce
Almejas en salsa

This recipe is popular in and around the port of Santander in northern Spain. Prawns or sliced squid can be substituted for the shellfish.

makes 20-24 tapa portions / serves 2 as a starter

500 g/1 lb clams in their shells (or cockles or mussels)
1 tablespoon olive oil
1 tablespoon chopped onion
1 garlic clove, chopped
2 tomatoes, skinned and chopped
1 teaspoon hot pimentón
1 wine glass of dry sherry
1 tablespoon chopped parsley
salt and pepper

Put the shellfish to soak for an hour or two in cold water so that they spit out any sand. Discard any which are cracked or that don't close when handled, or whose weight indicates that they are full of sand.

Warm the oil in a wide shallow pan (a wok is perfect). Throw in the onion and garlic, and let it fry gently for a few moments to take colour. Add the tomatoes and pimentón. Turn up the heat, stirring with a wooden spoon as the tomatoes soften.

Pour in the sherry and bubble up to evaporate the alcohol. Add the shellfish and turn them in the hot sauce until they open. Discard any that remain closed. Add the parsley. Taste and add salt and pepper.

Take them off the heat and serve one each per tapa, with a topping of the rich sauce.

Griddled razor shells
Navajas a la plancha

These are a neglected delicacy in Britain, even though razor shells are common enough round our shores. As a child, I used to find them on the beach and eat them raw. Griddled only long enough for them to open, they make a perfect little titbit for a tapa.

makes 12 tapa mouthfuls / serves 3 as a starter
12 razor shells
1 lemon, to serve

Soak the molluscs in cold water for an hour or two so that they spit out any sand.

Heat a griddle or heavy iron frying pan (skillet) until it is sizzling hot. Griddle the shellfish until they open in their own steam. Discard any that remain closed.

Remove them immediately from the heat. Serve one each as a tapa with a squeeze of lemon.

Basque crab
Changurro

The Basques make this with spider crab, *centolla*, caught off the coast of Guipuzcoa (and all round the coasts of Europe, including the Mediterranean). Spider crabs, as their name suggests, are spiky-bodied, long-legged creatures lacking the characteristic well-developed claws; their meat is deliciously succulent.

makes 21-24 tapa mouthfuls / serves 2 as a main course
1 large cooked crab or 175 g/6 oz prepared crab meat
4 tablespoons olive oil
1 small leek, chopped finely

1 tablespoon chopped onion
1 garlic clove, chopped
1 teaspoon hot pimentón
1 tablespoon tomato purée
1 small glass of dry sherry
1 tablespoon brandy
to finish
2 tablespoons fresh breadcrumbs
1 tablespoon chopped parsley
salt and pepper

Pick the crab meat from the shell (if necessary) and fork the dark and the white meat together.

Heat half the oil in a small pan and add the leek, onion and garlic and a tablespoon of water. Cook the vegetables gently until soft. Add the crab meat, stir to blend, and reheat. Add the pimentón, tomato purée, sherry and brandy and bubble up for a minute or two to evaporate the alcohol. Taste and adjust the seasoning.

Return the crab mixture to its shell, or spread in an earthenware cazuela or small gratin dish. At this point you can leave it or freeze it for later.

When you're ready to serve, sprinkle with breadcrumbs tossed with the parsley, trickle with the remaining oil and pop in a high oven or under a very hot grill for 5 minutes or so to crisp and brown the top. Serve in its cooking dish, with forks for sharing.

Spider crab with saffron dressing
Centolla a la vinagreta levantina

The spider crab, a clawless crustacean with a round spiky shell which is red even when uncooked, looks like an oversized daddy-long-legs. The meat is pure white and fine-flavoured but fiddly to extract – which, along with its unconventional looks, explains why, though plentiful in Atlantic waters, it's a neglected delicacy everywhere but on Mediterranean shores. It's eaten with mayonnaise, or plain with lemon, and in Valencia, it's sometimes served with a saffron-perfumed vinaigrette. To cook any crab from raw, start in cold salted water, bring gently to the boil, allow 5 minutes cooking time, leave to cool in its cooking water, then pull the two shells apart, leaving them hinged together, prop vertically and leave to drain.

serves 6 as a tapa / 2-3 as a starter

1 large or 2 smaller spider crabs, ready-cooked
4 tablespoons olive oil
1 onion, chopped finely
1 teaspoon hot pimentón or powdered chilli
6-8 saffron threads soaked in a splash of boiling water
1 small glass of brandy
1 teaspoon sherry- or wine vinegar
1 hard-boiled egg, chopped finely
salt

Separate the upper shell from the underparts, remove the whiskery little gills and click off the mouthpiece with its dark intestinal-tract, and chop the body straight down the line of each leg to give lollipop-like chunks, each with a leg attached.

Now make the dressing. Heat the oil in a small pan till just before it bubbles. Add the chopped onion, salt lightly and cook gently for a few minutes until it softens. Sprinkle in the pimentón or chilli and add the saffron with its soaking water and bubble up. Add the brandy and bubble up again till the steam no longer smells of alcohol. Remove the pan from the heat and stir in the vinegar and chopped hard-boiled egg. Check the seasoning.

Serve the vinaigrette as a dipping sauce with the crab lollipops, providing some kind of sharp instrument forks for poking out the little pockets of meat from the hard scraps of carapace.

MEAT

Pork remains the universal meat of Spain – the omnivorous pig has long been an honoured member of the Spanish rural household. As well as being allowed to range wild through the woods to scavenge for roots and acorns, he recycles the kitchen leftovers, making good use of edibles which would otherwise go to waste. The annual pig-killing still provides isolated farming communities with their winter supplies of salt-cured wind-dried ham and sausage.

In what was once Muslim Spain, which included Andalucía, pork was a dietary taboo until the Christian re-conquest at the end of the fifteenth century. Lamb and mutton, the preferred meat of the Moors, disappeared from the southern menu at that time, although the shepherding uplands continued to enjoy them. As recently as fifteen years ago in my local town of Tarifa, lamb was considered an unacceptably Moorish taste.

Kid is the great treat among the rural communities of the south. Roasted or as a savoury stew, it marks the high-spot of the country wedding feast, a roofing-out party (a son of housewarming party), or at any occasion where the food must be special.

Since Andalucía breeds fighting bulls for the ring, beef also figures on the tapa table. During the summer bullfighting season the little villages have a sudden glut of mature beef. Local bars and restaurants make the most of this cheap plenty. Such beef is not the most tender of morsels but the flavour is good, and *carne de lidia* (fighting beef)

Opposite: Grilled lamb cutlets

makes a fine slow-cooked stew. Tough meat from any part of the animal is often sliced into thin steaks – *filetes* – which are garlicked and flash-fried, Chinese-style.

For the rest, offal dishes are often served as tapas in bars and restaurants. Offal is the traditional source of cheap protein for the urban poor, who had no access to those wild harvests available to country people. Variety meats, such as tripe, liver, heart and kidneys, are familiar enough, but the tapa-hunting traveller will certainly come across stranger titbits – thyme-marinated cawl wrapped around vine twigs, and ears and tails and trotters stewed and spiced Moorish-style with cinnamon and cloves.

Meatballs in tomato sauce
Albóndigas en salsa

Moulding meatballs is one of the first culinary tasks Spanish children undertake – small neat fingers are perfect for working the paste and rolling the mixture into little marbles. The proportion of meat to breadcrumbs varies according to the means of the cook. Serve them as a main course, with rice or mashed potato. They can be made well ahead and reheated, and freeze beautifully in their sauce.

makes 10-12 meatballs / serves 2 as a main course
250 g/8 oz minced (ground) pork and/or beef
1 egg
2 tablespoons fresh breadcrumbs, soaked in a little water
1 garlic clove, chopped
1 tablespoon chopped parsley
½ teaspoon salt
1 tablespoon plain (all-purpose) flour
1 tablespoon olive oil
pepper

the sauce
1 onion, chopped

500 g/1 lb tomatoes, skinned and chopped (fresh or canned)
1 wine glass of dry sherry
1 bay leaf

Work the meat, egg, breadcrumbs, garlic and herbs together with the salt and plenty of pepper. Work it some more until the mixture is a firm ball of paste. Divide it into 10-12 marble-sized balls. Roll the balls lightly in the flour.

Heat the oil in a frying pan (skillet). Put in the meatballs and fry them gently for 5-6 minutes, turning them to cook all sides. Remove the meatballs and reserve them.

Now make the sauce. The meat will have released extra fat into the pan, so use that to fry the onion gently until it softens. Add the tomatoes and bubble up fiercely until you have a thick sauce. Add the sherry and bay leaf and heat again to evaporate the alcohol. Return the meatballs to the pan, lid and cook them gently in the sauce for 10-15 minutes.

Serve each meatball with a little sauce, spiked with a cocktail stick.

Grilled (broiled) spiced hamburgers
Hamburguesas a la plancha

This is the universal hamburger, spiced Spanish-style. It is really a flattened meatball, which is perhaps why it achieved instant popularity in Spain.

makes 8 bite-sized hamburgers

250 g/8 oz minced (ground) beef
2 tablespoons fresh breadcrumbs
1 garlic clove, finely chopped
1 tablespoon finely chopped onion
1 tablespoon chopped parsley
1 teaspoon ground cumin

1 small egg, forked to blend
a little olive oil for greasing
salt and pepper
bread and quartered lemons (to serve)

Work the minced (ground) meat, breadcrumbs, garlic, onion, parsley, cumin, egg and salt and pepper together with your hands, until you have a smooth, slightly sticky mass. Divide the mixture into 8 balls. Flatten them into thin discs.

Heat the griddle or a heavy iron frying pan (skillet). Slick it with the oil. When it is smoking, smack on the hamburgers. Cook them quickly, turning once. Slip them onto same-size rounds of bread toasted with a little olive oil.

Steaks with blue cheese
Filetes con cabrales

Butchers in Spain are expert at turning a whole beef carcass into fine-cut steaks – *filetes* – the cut most in demand by Spanish housewives. Meat is not jointed, but de-boned and separated into large pieces which follow the muscular structure of the animal. All but the toughest shin is then sliced up into thin steaks, Chinese-style, for flash-frying. This is a popular little tapa in northern Spain.

makes 4-6 tapa portions / serves 2-3 as a starter
250 g/8 oz very thin-cut lean braising steak
1 tablespoon olive oil
1 garlic clove, chopped finely
50 g/2 oz blue cheese, cubed (Cabrales, Roquefort or Stilton)
salt and pepper
bread squares to serve

Trim the steak into bite-sized pieces. Put it to marinate for 10-15 minutes in the olive oil, garlic and salt and pepper.

Heat up a griddle or heavy iron frying pan (skillet). Flash fry the steaks and put each on a square of bread which will just accommodate it.

Top each steak with a nugget of the blue cheese. Spike with a cocktail stick, and serve hot.

Breadcrumbed steaks
Filetes a la milanesa

This is an adaptable method of making a little of something good go further. Pork, veal or chicken can be used instead of beef, and I sometimes mix a pinch of dried thyme and a little hot pimentón into the coating crumbs if I think the meat lacks flavour. You can proceed as far as the egg-and-breadcrumbing and pop the coated *filetes* into the freezer, ready to be fried later.

makes 10 tapa portions / serves 2-3 as a main course
250 g/8 oz thin-cut beef steaks
2 heaped tablespoons seasoned bread flour
1 medium egg forked with its own volume of milk
4 tablespoons fine breadcrumbs
oil for frying (sunflower and olive oil mixed is excellent)
1 salt and pepper
lemon quarters, to serve

Using a wine bottle or rolling pin, flatten the steaks between 2 sheets of clingfilm till paper-thin. Cut into bite-sized strips and season with salt and pepper.

Spread the flour on one plate, the egg on a second, the breadcrumbs on a third. Dust the steaks through the flour, and then dip them in the egg so that both sides are lightly coated. Press them into the breadcrumbs to make an even jacket, shaking off any excess.

Heat enough oil to just submerge the steaks in a frying pan (skillet). When it is lightly hazed with blue (don't let it smoke), slip in the breadcrumbed fillets – not all at a time or the oil temperature will drop. Fry until the coating is golden brown and crisp, turning them once, and transfer to kitchen paper to drain. Continue until all are done. Serve with lemon quarters for squeezing.

Lamb ribs with pimentón
Frite de cordero

This dish of spicy lamb ribs is a speciality of Pedraza near Segovia on Spain's high central plateau. It makes a delicious main course served with rice or mashed potato. You can prepare it ahead as it reheats well and freezes perfectly.

makes 7-8 tapa portions / serves 3-4 as a starter
1 whole breast of lamb, cut into riblets
2 tablespoons olive oil
3 garlic cloves, crushed with 1 teaspoon salt
1 tablespoon pimentón
1 teaspoon dried oregano
1 tablespoon chopped parsley
1 tablespoon wine vinegar

Trim the excess fat from the lamb (not too much, this is a rich, oily little dish) and make sure all the pieces are bite-sized.

Heat the oil in a shallow casserole. Turn the meat pieces in the hot oil. Add the garlic and salt, and fry gently until everything takes a little colour. Stir in the paprika, herbs, vinegar and add a tumblerful of water.

Bring all to the boil, turn down the heat, lid tightly and leave to simmer very slowly for an hour or so, until the meat is tender and the juices have practically all cooked away. Remove the lid for the final 5 minutes and bubble up to evaporate any extra liquid. Drain off excess fat – lamb fat hardens very quickly.

Serve the riblets, one each per tapa, with plenty of bread to mop the fingers.

Grilled (broiled) lamb cutlets with garlic mayonnaise
Chuletas de cordero con ajioli

Spanish home-produced lamb is relatively small, giving cutlets of one single juicy bite. In my favourite tapa bar in Seville where these *chuletas* are a popular luxury tapa, the cook speeds up the grilling (broiling) with a red-hot flat-iron applied to the top side.

makes 6 tapa portions / serves 2 as a main course

6 baby lamb cutlets, neatly trimmed (keep the trimmings)
1 tablespoon olive oil
1 teaspoon dried oregano
sea salt and freshly-ground pepper

the sauce
6 tablespoons mayonnaise (page 38)
2 garlic cloves, crushed
bread, to serve

Remove excess fat and dice along with the trimmings. Rub the meat with olive oil, oregano and pepper and leave for at least 10 minutes to marinate. Fry the trimmings on a hot pan till the fat runs and keep on turning them over the heat till the bits are all exquisitely brown and crisp. Pop onto little bits of bread and serve hot as a little appetiser.

Meanwhile mix the mayonnaise with the crushed garlic.

Heat up the griddle, grill or barbecue. Grill (or broil) the cutlets over or under the fiercest heat possible, starting with the fat side towards the heat. The cutlets should be charred on the outside, but still pink and juicy within.

Serve one cutlet per tapa, with a spoonful of the garlic mayonnaise for dipping (see photo page 143).

Venison or beef in red wine
Guiso de venado o buey

This recipe for rich venison stew comes from a little *venta* (small country bar) on the road from Algeciras to Ronda, which skirts the great deer forest of Almoraima, once the largest private estate in Europe. The proprietor made good use of the bounty on his doorstep: the tender fillet was grilled over charcoal in the open fireplace, and the rest went into his famous aromatic *guiso*. The stew makes an excellent main dish, served with rice or baked potatoes. It can be prepared ahead, freezes perfectly, and is even better reheated.

makes 20-24 tapa mouthfuls /
serves 4-5 as a main course

1 kg/2 lb stewing venison (or beef), diced
2 tablespoons seasoned flour
4 tablespoons olive oil or pork dripping
2 tablespoons diced serrano ham or lean bacon
2 garlic cloves, chopped
1 medium onion, sliced into half-moons
1 carrot, scraped and diced
1 stick celery, diced
1 tablespoon pimentón (smoked for preference)
a dozen peppercorns, crushed
2 generous glasses red wine
2 bay leaves
1 sprig of thyme
sea salt

Trim the meat into bite-sized pieces and dust through the seasoned flour, coating lightly.

Heat the oil in a heavy casserole and fry the meat over a high heat until it takes a little colour, then push it to one side (or remove and reserve) and add the ham, garlic, onion, carrot and celery and cook them gently until they soften and brown a little. Stir in the pimentón

and peppercorns. Pour in the wine and bubble up. Add enough water to just submerge the meat, add the herbs and a little salt, and bring back to the boil.

Turn down the heat, lid tightly and leave to simmer very gently on the top of the stove (or in a low oven at Gas Mark 2/150°C/300°F) for 1-2 hours, until the meat is very tender. Check every now and then and add a little more water if necessary. Serve with plenty of bread – the juices are delicious.

Pork medallions with lemon and marjoram
Lomo de cerdo con limón y mejorana

The lemon cuts the natural richness of the pork in this simple recipe. It's a particularly good barbecue meat. Serve it as a main course with mashed potatoes or a well-flavoured juicy risotto.

makes 6 tapa portions / serves 2-3 as a main course
6 thin-cut pork medallions about the size of your hand
1 tablespoon olive oil
juice of 1 lemon
1 garlic clove, crushed
1 tablespoon marjoram
salt and pepper
rounds of bread, to serve

Rub the pork medallions with the oil, lemon juice, garlic, herbs, and salt and pepper. Leave them to marinate for at least 10 minutes.

Heat a griddle or heavy iron frying pan (skillet). Grill (broil) the medallions over a very high heat, turning once. Make sure they are cooked right through.

Serve each medallion on its own round of bread, spiked with a cocktail stick.

Tripe and chilli with chickpeas
Callos con garbanzos en salsa picante

In Spain, tripe is sold ready-scrubbed, but not yet cooked. This raw material gives the finished dish a much more glutinous, rich juice than if it is made with pre-cooked tripe. However, the chilli-spiked tomato-based sauce in this recipe gives the tripe back some of its flavour. It can be prepared well ahead. If you would like to freeze a portion, leave out the chickpeas – they can go in when you reheat it.

makes 15-20 tapa mouthfuls / serves 2 as a main course
250 g/8 oz ready-cooked tripe
1 small chorizo, or salami with 1 teaspoon paprika (optional)
2 tablespoons olive oil
1 onion, chopped
1 wine glass of dry sherry
500 g/1 lb tomatoes, skinned and chopped (fresh or canned)
1 bay leaf
1 teaspoon thyme
1 fresh or dried chilli, deseeded and chopped, or
½ teaspoon cayenne pepper
4 tablespoons cooked chickpeas (fresh or canned)
1 garlic clove, chopped finely
1 tablespoon chopped parsley
salt and pepper

Cut the tripe and the chorizo or salami, if used, into small bite-sized pieces.

Warm the olive oil in a shallow pan. Throw in the chopped onion and fry gently until soft. Add the tripe pieces, chorizo or salami and paprika if used, and the sherry. Bubble up to evaporate the alcohol.

Stir in the tomatoes, bay leaf, thyme and chilli or cayenne. Bring to the boil again, turn down the heat and simmer gently, uncovered, for 20-25 minutes, until the sauce is thick and rich. Stir in the chickpeas, garlic and parsley, and reheat. Cook for another 5 minutes. Taste and add salt and pepper.

Serve with forks and plenty of bread.

Marinated griddled pork fillet
Lomo en adobo a la plancha

Spanish housewives can buy sliced, ready-marinated fillets of pork from the butcher for this excellent fast food, which is popular as a tapa all over Spain. Served in a roll, it makes a satisfying lunchtime snack. It's the perfect meat for a barbecue. Make it in larger quantities for freezing after the marinating, ready for cooking as required.

makes 12-15 tapa portions / serves 3-4 as a light meal

250 g/8 oz pork fillet
1 heaped tablespoon pimentón
pinch dried oregano
pinch dried thyme
1 garlic clove, crushed with a little sea salt
1 tablespoon olive oil, plus extra for greasing
rounds of bread and lemon quarters, to serve

Dry the pork fillet, lay it on a clean cloth and rub it all over with a paste made with the pimentón, oregano, thyme, garlic and oil. Wrap it up in the foil, and leave it in a cool place overnight to take the flavours and develop a crust. It'll keep like this in the fridge for at least a week, improving all the time.

When you are ready to cook, cut the fillet into 8-10 thin medallions – on the diagonal if the fillet is slender.

Heat a griddle or heavy iron pan (skillet) until smoking hot. Oil it lightly. Smack on the pork medallions. Cook them for 5-6 minutes, turning once.

Serve each medallion on a round of bread (a slice of French stick, perhaps) which will just accommodate it. Accompany with quartered lemons.

Lamb's tongues in tomato sauce
Lenguas de cordero en salsa de tomate

The tongues can be prepared ahead, and reheated in the sauce when you are ready to serve. The dish makes a fine main course – serve it with baked potatoes and a salad. Ox tongue can be treated in the same way.

makes 15-20 tapa portions / serves 2-3 as a main course
3-4 lamb's tongues (fresh or from the brine pot)
1 large carrot, scraped and diced
1 medium onion, diced
1 celery stick, diced
1 bay leaf, crumbled
a dozen peppercorns, crushed
sea salt

the sauce
2 tablespoons olive oil
2 garlic cloves, crushed
500 g/1 lb tomatoes, skinned and chopped (fresh or canned)
1 wine glass of dry sherry
Pinch of thyme
salt and pepper

to serve
1 tablespoon toasted slivered almonds or pine kernels
small rounds of fried bread

Rinse the lamb's tongues. Put them in a saucepan with enough water to cover. Bring to the boil, skim and add the carrot, onion, celery, bay, peppercorns and salt. Lid and leave to simmer for about an hour, until the tongues are tender. Leave to cool in the cooking-water. When the tongues are cool enough to handle, slip off the thick skin – if the meat is tender, the skin comes off quite easily – and re-move any little bones. Cut the meat into slices.

Meanwhile make the sauce. Warm the oil in a small pan and throw in the garlic. Let it soften but don't let it brown. Add the toma-toes and bubble up, mashing with a fork till thick and smooth. Add the sherry and bubble up to evaporate the alcohol. Stir in the thyme and a ladleful of the cooking-water. Cook over a gentle heat until you have a thick sauce. Taste and add salt and pepper.

Lay the tongue slices in the sauce and reheat gently till bubbling. Serve each slice on a piece of fried bread, with a little of the sauce spooned over, and a few slivered almonds or pine kernels on top.

Veal kidneys with sherry
Riñones al jerez

Kidneys cooked in sherry, along with the tortilla (page 94), is the dish most frequently found in Andalucía's tapa bars. Cheap and delicious, it is easy to prepare, can be reheated quickly and freezes well. Serve it as a main course, with rice or mashed potatoes – I love it with chipped potatoes fried in olive oil (page 78).

makes 15-20 tapa mouthfuls / serves 2 as a main course

1 veal or 2 pork kidneys, trimmed and diced
1 tablespoon sherry (or wine) vinegar
2 tablespoons olive oil or pork dripping
1 large onion, slivered into half-moons
1 garlic clove, crushed
1 wine glass of dry sherry
1 tablespoon pimentón
1 tablespoon fresh white breadcrumbs
1 tablespoon chopped parsley
salt and pepper

Set the kidney pieces to soak in a bowl of water with vinegar for 20-30 minutes to neutralise the ammoniac taste. Drain and pat dry. Warm the oil or dripping in a casserole and gently fry the onion and garlic till soft. Add the kidney pieces and turn them in the hot oil. Add the sherry and bubble up to evaporate the alcohol. Add a glass of water, stir and bring back to the boil.

Turn down the heat, lid loosely and simmer gently for 25-30 min-

utes, until the kidneys are tender and the juices well reduced. Stir in the pimentón, breadcrumbs and parsley and reheat till bubbling. Taste and add salt and pepper.

Serve as a tapa in small portions, with a fork each and plenty of bread to mop up the delicious juices.

Note: this dish also works wonderfully well made with chicken livers.

Roast pork and potato crisps
Pata de cerdo al horno con patatas fritas

Big-city tapa bars with a high turnover often take pride in displaying a fine cold roast leg of pork cut to order as a luxury tapa. In my local bar by the port in Algeciras, it was the Saturday special, served on freshly-made potato crisps supplied from a frying-kiosk on the pavement outside. You can adapt the recipe for the leftovers from the Sunday joint.

makes 6 tapa portions / serves 2-3 as a starter
6 thin slices of roast pork
6 handfuls freshly-made lightly salted potato crisps
1 garlic clove, sliced
1 tablespoon olive oil
sea salt

Lay each slice of roast pork on its little bed of crisps.

Soften the garlic in the olive oil and sprinkle over the meat.

Finish with a good pinch of sea salt.

Griddled marinated lamb's kidneys
Riñones a la plancha

Lamb's kidneys make a perfect bite-sized tapa, while the marination in lemon and herbs gives a deliciously Mediterranean flavour.

makes 12 tapa portions / serves 4 as a starter
6 lamb's kidneys, skinned and halved lengthways
juice of 1 lemon
1 garlic clove, chopped
2 tablespoons olive oil
1 teaspoon dried oregano
1 tablespoon chopped parsley
salt and pepper
bread rounds and lemon quarters, to serve

Remove the fatty little core in each kidney half. Put the kidneys to marinate for at least 10 minutes in the lemon juice, garlic, oil, herbs and salt and pepper.

Preheat a griddle or heavy iron pan (skillet) or barbecue or grill. Cook the kidneys over or under a fierce heat, turning once. They should be charred outside, but still pink and juicy inside.

Serve on small rounds of bread accompanied by quarters of lemon.

Moorish kebabs
Pinchitos moruños

These little kebabs are a great feria treat in Andalucía. In Algeciras, my home town for ten years, feria was at the end of June, and it always rained for at least two of the carnival's five days. Each year the same fez-hatted *pinchito* (kebab) man took up temporary residence at one end of a beer and wine wholesaler's pavement bar. We would order cold half bottles of dry sherry from the wine merchant, and negotiate separately for the delicious Moroccan-spiced *pinchitos*, grilled over a charcoal-fuelled barbecue. The *pinchitos* came on long steel knitting-needles which we were honour-bound to return.

makes 8 kebabs / serves 4 as a starter
250 g/8 oz diced pork or lamb (offal is permissable)
2 tablespoons olive oil
1 tablespoon hot pimentón

1 teaspoon powdered saffron or turmeric
1 teaspoon cumin seeds
1 teaspoon dried thyme
1 teaspoon crushed garlic
8 cubes of bread, to serve

Check over the meat – all the pieces should be neatly trimmed and no bigger than ordinary dice – and mix well with the rest of the ingredients. Leave in a cool place overnight to take the flavours.

Next day, thread the meat on to 8 thin skewers leaving a little space between and allowing 6-7 little pieces per skewer.

Heat the grill or barbecue. Grill (or broil) the *pinchitos* over a very high heat, turning them frequently, until singed and cooked through but still juicy.

Serve hot on their skewers, with a cube of bread speared on the end.

Spiced casserole of lamb or kid
Caldereta de cordero o chivo

This method of thickening a stew with breadcrumbs and liver was common in medieval cookery. The recipe is from Malaga, where Moorish culinary influences remain strong.

makes 12-15 tapa portions / serves 3-4 as a main course
500 g/1 lb boned-out shoulder of lamb or kid
1 wine glass of sherry
a sprig of thyme
1 bay leaf
6 tablespoons olive oil
125 g/4 oz lamb's liver (in 1 piece)
2 garlic cloves, crushed with a little salt
2 tablespoons fresh breadcrumbs
juice and grated zest of 1 lemon
finely-chopped parsley for finishing
salt and pepper

Trim the meat into bite-sized pieces. Pack the pieces into a saucepan with the sherry, herbs and just enough water to cover the meat. Bring to the boil, skim, add the oil, turn down the heat, and simmer for 20 minutes. Add the liver to the pan, bring back to the boil, turn down to simmer and cook for 15 minutes till the liver is firm and cooked right through. Test the meat for tenderness – if it's not yet soft, continue to cook.

Meanwhile chop the liver and put it in a blender with the garlic and salt, breadcrumbs, a generous pinch of pepper and a ladleful of the cooking liquor from the meat. Process till smooth and reserve until the meat is tender – you may need to add a little water if it looks like drying out.

When the meat is done, stir in the liver purée, reheat and simmer gently for another 10 minutes. Take off the heat and stir in the lemon juice. Serve in individual earthenware casseroles, with a dusting of chopped parsley and grated lemon zest to finish.

Casserole of lamb or kid with saffron
Caldereta de cordero o chivo con azafran

This is a succulent way with a shoulder of lamb. If you use kid, the juices will be stickier and richer. You can prepare it in advance and reheat for serving. Make double quantities: it freezes beautifully.

makes 20-24 tapa portions / serves 2-3 as a main dish
1 small shoulder of lamb or kid, chopped into portions
through the bone
3 tablespoons olive oil
1 large onion, sliced
4 garlic cloves, chopped
1 wine glass of white wine or dry sherry
1 wine glass of water
1 bay leaf
12 saffron threads, soaked in a tablespoon boiling water
1 lemon, sliced thinly

1 short length cinnamon bark
salt and pepper
fried bread, to serve

Trim the lamb or kid into bite-sized pieces, bones and all. Heat the oil in a casserole which will comfortably accommodate the meat. Turn the pieces in the hot oil until they take a little colour. Push the meat to one side and fry the onion and garlic in the oil. Pour in the wine and bubble all up. Add the water, bay leaf, saffron with its water, lemon slices, cinnamon and salt and pepper.

Bring all back to the boil. Turn down the heat and lid tightly. Simmer gently on top of the stove (or in the oven at Gas Mark 2/150°C/300°F) for 1-1¼ hours, until the meat is tender and falling off the bone.

To serve as a tapa, heap on little squares of fried bread. As a main course, it's good with plain-cooked white rice, *arroz en blanco*, scattered with a handful of toasted almonds or pinenuts.

Cinnamon-spiced oxtail stew
Estofado de rabo de buey con canela

This rich Moorish-spiced stew is a speciality of Cordoba. Oxtail always features on the menu in leather-working areas, an industry for which Cordoba has long been world famous. The skins for the trade come in with the tail of the animal still attached, affording a tasty free morsel for the leather-worker's pot. The stew is better when reheated, and freezes perfectly.

makes 15-20 tapa portions / serves 3-4 as a main course
1 whole oxtail, divided into sections
2 tablespoons olive oil
1 tablespoon diced serrano ham or lean bacon
1 large onion, slivered
2 garlic cloves crushed with 1 teaspoon salt
1 celery stick, chopped
1 large carrot, scraped and diced

1 tablespoon pimentón
1 heaped tablespoon ground cinnamon
1 teaspoon crushed peppercorns
½ teaspoon powdered cloves
1 bay leaf
2 wine glasses of red wine

Wipe and trim the oxtail, discarding any excess fat.

Heat the oil in a casserole which will comfortably accommodate all the pieces. Turn the oxtail in the hot oil. Remove and reserve. Add the onion, garlic, celery and carrot and fry gently until the vegetables soften.

Return the oxtail to the pot, reheat and add the aromatics and the red wine. Bubble up, add 2 glasses of water and bring back to the boil. Turn down the heat, lid tightly and leave to cook on a very low heat (or in the oven at Gas Mark 2/150°C/300°F) for 3-4 hours, until the meat is practically falling off the bones. Check from time to time, and add more water if necessary.

Serve the stew in its dish, with small forks for sharing and chunks of soft-crumbed bread for mopping.

Grilled (broiled) pig's trotters with garlic and parsley
Patas de cerdo con ajo y perejil

Pig's trotters are much appreciated throughout Iberia as an addition to the beanpot. As a dish in their own right, they need nothing more than long slow cooking to soften them – otherwise preparation time is minimal. The trotters can be prepared ahead and grilled (broiled) when you are ready.

makes 16 tapa portions / serves 2-3 as a main course

4 pig's trotters, split lengthways
1 large onion, chunked
1 large carrot, scraped and chunked

1-2 bay leaves
½ teaspoon peppercorns
a dozen allspice berries
1 wine glass of sherry
2-3 tablespoons fresh breadcrumbs
1 tablespoon chopped parsley
1 garlic clove, chopped
2 tablespoons olive oil
salt and pepper

Rinse the pig's trotters and scrub them well. Tie them together in pairs, cut side against cut side. Pack them into a roomy pan which will just accommodate them, along with the onion, carrot, bay, peppercorns and allspice. Pour in the sherry and enough water to submerge the trotters generously. Add a teaspoon of salt.

Bring to the boil, skim, turn down the heat and simmer steadily for half an hour. Top up with boiling water to ensure the trotters are submerged, turn down the heat, lid tightly and leave to cook very gently for 4-5 hours, until the trotters are soft and the bones are dropping out. Check the water level every now and then, and add boiling water.

Let the trotters cool in their liquid. Remove and drain. Untie them and arrange in a grill pan cut-side up. Sprinkle with the breadcrumbs, parsley, garlic and salt and pepper, and finish with a trickle of oil.

Reheat in the oven, and then slip them under a blazing hot grill to gild and crisp the topping.

Liver pâté
Pastel de hígado

This is a useful standby for the tapa table which can be eaten hot or cold. It freezes well and can be prepared well ahead. As a main dish, serve hot with potatoes in winter, cold with a salad in summer.

makes 8-10 tapa portions / serves 4-6 as a starter
500 g/1 lb pig's liver
175 g/6 oz lean pork
2 tablespoons diced serrano ham, including plenty of fat
1 wine glass of white wine
1 tablespoon chopped parsley
1 tablespoon chopped onion
1 garlic clove, chopped
2 tablespoons olive oil or pork-dripping
1 egg, forked to blend
grated rind of 1 lemon
2 tablespoons fresh white breadcrumbs
1 bay leaf
sea salt and pepper

Preheat the oven to Gas Mark 4/180°C/350°F.

Mince the liver, pork and ham together; then mix in the wine and parsley and plenty of pepper. Fry the onion and garlic together in a tablespoon of oil or dripping until they soften, then fork the contents of the pan with the meat mixture. Work in the egg, lemon zest and breadcrumbs – use your hands, the most useful of kitchen implements.

Rub a small baking dish (large enough to accommodate the meats if filled right to the top) with the rest of the oil or dripping. Pack in the meat, top with the bay leaf and cover with foil.

Cook in the oven for 1-1½ hours, until the juices run clear when you test with a skewer pushed in the middle.

To serve hot, cut the pâté into bite-sized squares and accompany with chunks of bread. To serve cold, press under a weight overnight and serve with crisp lettuce leaves and spiced green olives (see p.12).

CHICKEN AND GAME

Throughout Spain chicken is an important source of protein. The housewives of a peasant-farming community keep hens primarily for eggs, but the young cockerels are fattened up for the pot. Small and well-flavoured, chicken remains a Sunday treat in rural communities, and a delectable addition to the tapa table on special occasions. Often combined with well-flavoured pot-herbs and vegetables, both to bulk up the meat and add flavour, one chicken can be made to feed a surprising number of people. Everything goes into the pot – including the neck and giblets – while the head and feet are carefully scrubbed and consigned to the simmering soup cauldron. Spanish housewives make up their own broth with vegetables and leftover bones. This gives added flavour and aroma to many dishes.

To make your own chicken (or fish stock), boil a chicken carcass (or 500 g/1 lb fish bones and heads) in 600 ml/1 pint/ 2½ cups water, with an onion, carrot, celery stick, bay leaf, a few black peppercorns and a little salt. Strain and use as required.

Game is plentiful in Spain's forests and plains – rabbits and small birds, snails and, particularly in the Levante, frogs, are a bounty still to be collected from the wild.

All these relatively lean meats benefit from a preliminary marination in olive oil, wine and herbs characteristic of the Spanish culinary tradition.

Opposite: Spiced grilled chicken

Spiced grilled chicken
Pollo en adobo a la plancha

This marinaded chicken was my children's favourite birthday bar-·
becue when we all lived in Spain. They could do the preparation
themselves – from spicing the chicken to building the fire over
which we balanced a makeshift barbecue made with a grid from the
oven resting on a few bricks.

makes 12 tapa portions / serves 2-3 as a main course

750 g/1½ lb chicken joints
2 tablespoons olive oil
1-2 garlic cloves, peeled and crushed
½ lemon, chunked
1 tablespoon hot or mild pimentón (smoked for preference)
1 tablespoon dried oregano
1 teaspoon cumin seeds
1 teaspoon crushed coriander seeds
1 teaspoon fine sea salt
½ teaspoon freshly ground black pepper

Chop the chicken joints into a dozen bite-sized pieces – get your
butcher to cooperate, or do it yourself with a heavy knife tapped
through the bones with a hammer. Put the chicken pieces in a
roomy bowl with the rest of the ingredients, turning to ensure everything is well-mixed, and leave all to marinade for a few hours
(overnight is even better).

When you're ready to cook, brush off the loose bits of marinade.

Grill (broil) the chicken pieces over or under a steady heat, making sure they're cooked right through (this is more easily done when
the pieces are bite-sized). The result should be deliciously charred
outside but remain juicy within (see photo page 167).

Chicken with red peppers
Pollo chilindron

This succulent dish from Zaragoza in Aragon is also prepared with the region's small, lean mountain lamb. You can replace the pimentón with a couple of *ñoras* – bell-shaped dried red peppers which are either torn into pieces for inclusion in a dish such as this, or soaked and scraped for their crimson pulp.

12 tapa portions / serves 3-4 as a main dish
750 g/1½ lb chicken joints
4 tablespoons olive oil
4-5 garlic cloves, roughly chopped
3 tablespoons diced serrano ham or lean bacon
1-2 tablespoons mild pimentón
1 teaspoon hot pimentón or powdered chilli
2-3 red peppers, de-seeded and cut into strips
500 g/1 lb ripe tomatoes, skinned and chopped
salt and pepper

Chop the chicken joints into bite-sized pieces by tapping a heavy knife firmly across the bone with a hammer (sounds brutal, but it works): divide drumsticks into 2, thighs into 2, wings into 2, breast into 4.

Heat the oil in a deep casserole. Put in the chicken pieces, garlic and onion and cook them gently until both meat and vegetables have taken a little colour. Push to one side (or remove and reserve) and add the ham and the pepper strips. Fry till the peppers soften and caramelise a little. Sprinkle in the pimentón and/or chilli powder, add the tomato pulp and bubble it all up, mashing with a fork. If necessary, return the chicken pieces to the sauce.

Turn down the heat, lid tightly and simmer for 25-30 minutes until the chicken is tender and the sauce well-reduced. Remove the lid at the end of the cooking time and bubble up to concentrate the juices. Taste and add salt and pepper.

Serve as a tapa on individual saucers, with bread for mopping fingers as well as the sauce.

Chicken with plenty of garlic
Pollo al ajillo

The classic Andaluz country housewife's way with a young barnyard cockerel or a rabbit from the rosemary-scented cistus scrub, this recipe depends on perfect raw ingredients. It's my family's favourite chicken dish and makes an excellent main course.

makes 10 tapa portions / serves 3-4 as a main dish
750 g/1½ lb chicken or rabbit joints
1 heaped tablespoon seasoned flour
8 tablespoons olive oil (no other oil will do)
a whole garlic head, skinned and roughly chopped
1 wine glass dry sherry
salt and pepper

Chop up the joints into bite-sized pieces as in the previous recipe, and dust with seasoned flour.

Heat the olive oil in a heavy frying pan or skillet – don't let it overheat. Put in the chicken and garlic and turn the pieces in the hot oil until they are well browned. Pour in the sherry and bubble it up.

Turn down the heat, lid loosely and leave to simmer gently on a low heat for 20-30 minutes, until the chicken is cooked through but still moist and tender, and the juices have practically all evaporated, leaving a deliciously garlicky oil as the sauce.

Serve with forks and plenty of bread.

Turkey with almonds and saffron
Pavo en pepitoria

The turkey was imported to Spain from the New World along with such staples as the potato, tomato, all the haricot beans (green, white, black, brown, red and speckled) and all the salad peppers including chilli. It's hard to imagine what Europe ate before Columbus made landfall.

15-20 tapa mouthfuls / serves 2 as a main dish
500 g/1 lb boned-out turkey meat
2 tablespoons olive oil or pork-dripping
1 thick slice day-old bread, crumbled
1 heaped tablespoon blanched almonds, crushed
1 tablespoon finely-chopped parsley
½ teaspoon powdered cloves
½ teaspoon powdered cinnamon
1 tablespoon hot pimentón (smoked for preference)
a dozen saffron threads soaked in 1 tablespoon
boiling water
1 tablespoon lemon juice
1 tablespoon chopped onion

Cut the turkey meat into bite-sized pieces.

Heat a tablespoon of oil and fry the bread, almonds and garlic until golden. Stir in the parsley and the dry spices. Transfer the contents of the pan to the food processor or use a pestle and mortar. Process or pound all to a thick sauce with the saffron and its soaking water and the lemon juice, adding a glass of water to make a little sauce.

Reheat the pan with the rest of the oil and gently fry the turkey pieces and the onion. When the turkey is a little browned and the onions are soft, stir in the sauce. Bubble up and then lid and turn down the heat. Simmer gently until the turkey is cooked – about 10-15 minutes. Add a little more water if the sauce looks like drying out. Serve at room temperature, with forks for sharing.

Breadcrumbed spiced chicken
Pollo rebozado

Spicy morsels of breadcrumbed chicken make delightful party tapas. For a main dish, use a whole jointed chicken, back and all, chopped into bite-sized pieces but with the bones left in – it'll yield 6 full portions.

8 tapa mouthfuls / serves 2 as a main course
350 g/12 oz boneless chicken
2 tablespoons seasoned flour
1 egg beaten with 1 tablespoon milk
4 heaped tablespoons fine breadcrumbs
1 tablespoon pimentón
1 teaspoon dried thyme
1 teaspoon freshly-ground pepper
olive oil for frying
salt and pepper

Cut the chicken into walnut-sized nuggets. Put the chicken and the seasoned flour in a bag and shake them up to coat lightly with flour. Shake off any excess.

Dip the nuggets in the egg-and-milk and then roll them in the breadcrumbs seasoned with pimentón, thyme and freshly-ground pepper.

In a frying pan (skillet), heat enough oil to just submerge the chicken pieces. Wait till it's lightly hazed with blue and slip in the chicken pieces, a few at time so that the oil temperature remains high. Fry gently, turning the pieces once, until the coating is crisp and the meat firm (test with your finger). The oil should not be too hot as the chicken must be thoroughly cooked by the time the breadcrumbs are browned.

Drain on kitchen paper, and serve spiked with cocktail sticks.

Deep-fried quails with garlic
Codornices con ajo

While farmed quail have now replaced small birds from the wild on the Spanish menu, recipes still reflect what was once poor-folks' food. In the beachside bar at Punta Paloma near Tarifa, for many years my local market town, the birds were spatchcocked – a method which allows them to cook fast – and dropped into the frying-vat.

makes 4 large tapa portions / serves 2 as a main course
4 quail
sherry
4 garlic cloves, chopped roughly
oil for deep-frying
salt and pepper

Spatchcock the birds by splitting them right down the back, from vent to neck, then flatten them firmly with your hand – like squashed frogs – and push a skewer through the legs to keep the shape. Sprinkle with sherry, garlic, salt and pepper and leave for a few hours. Drain and pat dry.

Heat enough oil to submerge the birds completely. When the surface is lightly hazed with blue, slip them in one at a time, allowing the oil to reheat between each addition. The oil will spit, so be careful. Fry the birds until the skin and all the little bones are brown and crisp.

Sprinkle with salt and serve on thick slices of fresh bread.

Quails with parsley and garlic
Codornices a la bilbaina

Farmed quail provide a succulent replacement for the *chimbos* – all manner of little songbirds – which were prepared to this recipe from Bilbao.

makes 4 tapa portions / serves 2 as a main course
4 quail
2 tablespoons olive oil
2 tablespoons unsalted butter
2 heaped tablespoons fresh breadcrumbs
1 garlic clove, chopped
2 heaped tablespoons chopped parsley
salt and pepper

Halve the birds and season with salt and pepper.

Heat the oil and butter in a heavy frying pan (skillet) until it foams. Put in the birds skin-side down and fry them gently, turning once, until they are golden brown all over and cooked right through – about 10 minutes in all. Remove to a hot serving dish.

Stir the breadcrumbs, garlic and parsley into the oily drippings and fry till crisp and brown. Top the birds with this fragrant topping and serve them hot. Eat with your fingers – no one can eat small birds with a knife and fork.

Spiced pigeons
Pichones a la toledana

In this recipe from the great walled city of Toledo on Spain's central plateau, the spicy sweet-sour sauce perfectly balances the gamey flavour of the pigeons.

makes 16 tapa portions / serves 4 as a main course

8 tablespoons olive oil
4 pigeons, cleaned and quartered
2 large onions, slivered into half-moons
16 whole unskinned garlic cloves
1 tablespoon diced serrano ham or lean bacon
2 wine glasses of dry sherry
1 tablespoon sherry- or wine vinegar
2 bay leaves
1 short length cinnamon stick
2-3 cloves, crushed
salt and pepper

Heat the oil in a heavy casserole. Put in the pigeon quarters and turn them in the hot oil. Add the slivered onion, garlic cloves and ham or bacon and fry gently till the onion softens and gilds a little. Pour in the sherry and the vinegar. Add the cinnamon, cloves and bay, season with salt and pepper, and pour in just enough water to barely submerge everything.

Bring all to the boil, turn down the heat, lid tightly and leave to simmer for 40-50 minutes, until the pigeons are quite tender.

Take off the lid towards the end and evaporate the juices, leaving the pigeons bathed in aromatic oil.

Serve each quarter with bread. Make sure each person has a garlic clove – creamy and gently-flavoured when slow-cooked like this. Pop it straight into your mouth from its papery covering.

Chicken kebabs with fresh tomato sauce
Pinchos de polio con salsa picada

Chicken breasts marinated in oil, garlic, marjoram and lemon have a deliciously sharp flavour. This is a good meat for the barbecue. Serve it with rice and a salad as a main dish in the summer.

makes 8 tapa portions / serves 2 as a main course
2 boneless chicken breasts
2 tablespoons olive oil
1 garlic clove, crushed
1 tablespoon lemon juice
1 tablespoon chopped marjoram or oregano
8 cubes of bread
salt and pepper
1 small glass of water

the sauce
1 tablespoon finely-chopped onion
2 tablespoons finely-chopped cucumber
3 tablespoons finely-chopped tomato
1 tablespoon sherry- or wine vinegar
1 tablespoon fresh breadcrumbs

Divide the chicken breasts lengthways into 4, giving 8 pieces in all. Skewer the strips lengthways. Put them to marinate for a few hours in the oil, garlic, lemon and marjoram or oregano, with a seasoning of salt and pepper.

Mix all the sauce ingredients together and leave them in a cool place to marry the flavours and swell the breadcrumbs.

Grill (or broil) the skewers on a barbecue, griddle or under the grill. Serve with a spoonful of sauce per skewer, with a bread cube speared on the end of each one.

Sweet and sour rabbit
Cochefrito de conejo

A speciality of the elegant city of Cordoba, once the capital of Al-Andazu, the dish is also very good made with lamb or kid. Serve it with baked potatoes as a winter main course, or with rice and a salad in the summer.

makes 10-12 tapa portions / serves 3-4 as a main course
750 g/1½ lb rabbit joints
1 teaspoon cracked peppercorns
½ teaspoon sea salt
6 tablespoons olive oil
2-3 garlic cloves, crushed
1 tablespoon raisins, soaked to swell
1 tablespoon sherry- or wine vinegar

Chop the rabbit joints into at least a dozen bite-sized pieces and toss them with the salt and pepper. Heat the oil in a casserole and add the rabbit and garlic. Fry until the meat takes a little colour. Add the raisins, vinegar and enough water to just submerge the rabbit pieces.

Bring all to the boil, turn down the heat, cover, and leave to simmer for 30-40 minutes or till the meat is perfectly tender, uncovering the pot for the final few minutes till the sauce is little more than a coating of sweet-sour aromatic oil.

Serve one piece per tapa portion, with chunks of bread.

Rabbit with chocolate
Conejo a la ampurdanesa

One of the most famous and delightful dishes of the Spanish kitchen, this is a direct result of Spanish involvement in Mexico, where chocolate was used as a spice, as here. In its original powdered form it was also – once sweetened, spiced with chilli and flavoured with vanilla – the imperial drink of the Aztec Emperor. Cook it ahead and reheat when you're ready to serve.

makes 12 tapa portions / serves 3-4 as a main course
750 g/1½ lb rabbit joints
2 tablespoons seasoned flour
1 tablespoon diced ham fat or streaky bacon
12 pickling onions or small shallots
2 wine glasses of red wine
2 tablespoons ground hazelnuts or almonds
2 tablespoons unsweetened cocoa powder
1 teaspoon powdered cinnamon
salt and pepper

Divide the rabbit joints into a dozen bite-sized pieces and toss them in the seasoned flour, shaking off excess. In a heavy casserole, fry the ham or bacon until the fat runs. Add the rabbit pieces and the onions and turn them in the hot fat to take colour (you may need a little extra pork-dripping or oil).

Pour in the wine and allow it to bubble up for a minute or two till the steam no longer smells of alcohol. Add a glass of water, bubble up again, turn down the heat, lid tightly and simmer gently for 20-30 minutes, until the meat is tender but not yet dropping off the bone.

You may need to add a little more water if looks like drying out.

Stir in the ground nuts, cocoa powder and cinnamon and cook gently uncovered for another 10 minutes or so, until the sauce is smooth, dark and thick. Taste and adjust the seasoning – you might need a little sugar. Serve one piece per tapa, with a little sauce and a hunk of bread.

Potted game
Morteruelo

This is much like English potted meats, of which it may well be the ancestor. Royal marriages in medieval times brought Spanish princesses and their cooks and culinary habits to the courts of England.

makes 8-10 tapa portions / serves 4-6 as a starter

500 g/1 lb ready-cooked game meat (partridge, hare, rabbit)
250 g/8 oz veal or chicken livers (or saved from the game)
2 tablespoons diced fatty bacon (tocino)
1 wine glass of dry sherry
1 tablespoon mild pimentón (smoked for preference)
1 teaspoon cracked peppercorns
1 teaspoon ground cinnamon
½ teaspoon ground cloves
2 tablespoons toasted pine kernels or slivered almonds
salt

Pick over the game, discarding any bones and skin. Cook the liver till tender in a small pan with the diced bacon, sherry, spices, salt and just enough water to cover.

Put the game meat, liver and bacon into a blender with the toasted nuts, and process with enough of the cooking liquid to give a thick soft paste. Taste and add salt and pepper. Pot and leave to cool.

Serve with hot bread.

Snails in tomato sauce
Caracoles en salsa

Snails are a popular tapa in small village bars and the less affluent corners of cities – not least because the ingredients can be gathered free from the countryside. Two kinds are collected for the table: caracoles, the large brown-shelled variety familiar from the snail recipes of France and which are gathered year-round, and caracolitos, tiny snails no bigger than a thumbnail with delicately-speckled grey and gold shells which aestivate on dried-out thistles through the summer and are available from the end of May through June.

makes 20-24 tapa portions / serves 4 as a starter
4 tablespoons olive oil
1 onion, sliced finely
1 tablespoon pimentón (hot or mild, smoked for preference)
500 g/1 lb tomatoes, skinned, de-seeded and chopped
2 bay leaves
1-2 thyme sprigs
500 g/1 lb ready-cooked snails in shells
1 tablespoon toasted breadcrumbs
1 tablespoon chopped parsley
salt and pepper

Heat 3 tablespoons of the oil in a shallow pan and gently fry the onion for a few moments. Add the paprika, tomatoes and bouquet garni. Bubble up to soften the tomatoes and thicken the sauce. Add the snails. Simmer all together for 20 minutes, until the sauce and the snails are well married. Taste and add salt and pepper.

Transfer to individual cazuelas – shallow earthenware casseroles – or little gratin dishes, top each portion with a little hat of breadcrumbs and parsley and finish with a trickle of the remaining oil. Flash under the grill to gild the topping. Serve hot, with cocktail sticks to hook the snails from their shells, and plenty of bread to mop up the juices.

Snails with ham and chorizo
Caracoles a la burgalesa

This is how they like their snails in the northern city of Burgos – a town which also has a reputation for fresh white curd cheese and delicious junket.

makes 20-24 tapa portions / serves 4 as a starter
4 tablespoons olive oil
2 garlic cloves, chopped
1 tablespoon diced serrano ham or lean bacon
1 fresh chorizo, skinned and mashed
1 tablespoon fresh breadcrumbs
1 tablespoon hot pimentón or powdered chilli
1 wine glass of white wine
500 g/1 lb ready-cooked snails in their shells
1 tablespoon chopped parsley
salt and pepper

Heat the oil in a frying pan (skillet). Add the garlic and let it fry for a few moments to soften. Add the diced ham or bacon and chorizo and fry till the fat runs. Stir in the breadcrumbs, sprinkle with pimentón or chilli, and fry for another minute or two till the fat has all been absorbed. Add the wine, bubble up to evaporate the alcohol, then tip in the snails. Turn them in the hot sauce and bubble up. Turn down the heat, lid and cook gently for 20 minutes or so to develop all the flavours. Finish with the chopped parsley.

Serve with forks and plenty of bread.

Frogs' legs in waterproof jackets
Ancas de rana en gabardina

While frogs are no longer wild-gathered food for free, Spain's Levante region shares a taste for frogs' legs with its northern neighbours, the French. This recipe is from Albuferia, where the marshes once harboured a plentiful supply of the raw materials.

makes 8 tapa portions / serves 2 as a starter

4 pairs of frogs' legs, separated
2 tablespoons dry sherry
1 teaspoon lemon juice
1 teaspoon thyme
1 garlic clove, chopped
1 tablespoon olive oil
2 tablespoons seasoned flour
3-4 tablespoons fresh breadcrumbs
1 tablespoon chopped parsley
1 large egg
salt
oil for frying
lemon quarters, to serve

Put the frogs' legs to marinate for an hour or so in the sherry, lemon juice, thyme, garlic and a tablespoon of the olive oil.

Spread the seasoned flour on one plate and the breadcrumbs mixed with the parsley on another. Fork up the egg with its own volume of water in another.

Drain the frogs' legs and pat dry. Dust them through the flour, dip in the egg and then press into the breadcrumbs.

Heat enough oil in a frying pan (skillet) to just submerge the frogs' legs. Wait till a faint blue haze rises and slip in the coated legs, a few at a time, and fry until the coating is crisp and golden. Serve with lemon quarters.

CROQUETTES, PASTIES AND PIES

These little snacks are a way of stretching small quantities of expensive ingredients, such as chicken and ham, prawns and shrimps, even a piece of well-flavoured cheese. Croquettes are a standby of Andaluz housewives, while pasties and pies are more frequently to be found in the northern provinces of Spain, particularly Galicia.

The Gallegos, while their language has long vanished, are skilled bakers, sharing something of a common culinary heritage with the other Celtic nations of Europe, including the Welsh and the Scots. Their pastry, however, is not primarily designed to be crisp and might be considered more like a pizza dough than a pie-crust, although there is no reason why you shouldn't use your own favourite shortcrust or puff pastry if you wish. Spain does indeed have a repertoire of fat-shortened pastries, both short and puff, but these are normally used for sweet things rather savoury, such as the shortbread-like *mantecados* and cinnamon-flavoured *polverones* of Christmas. Northern cooks prefer the baking oven to the southerners' open flame. Which leaves the cooks of Andalucía pre-eminent in the art of frying, learning at mother's elbow how to form a neat little croquette from a ladleful of flour-thickened sauce which can be made with the broth from the cocido and flavoured with whatever you please, jacket it with breadcrumbs and fry it at just the right

Opposite: Shrimp croquettes

temperature to turn it into a crisp little mouthful of happiness. Croquettes are always served piping hot from the frying pan (skillet) with a glass of chilled wine, while pies and pasties are usually eaten warm or at room temperature as a quick snack at any time of day or night and might, in their place of origin, come with a cooling glass of cider or red wine.

Shrimp croquettes
Croquetas de gambas

Shrimps are the classic filling for *croquetas* in the sea-front bars and *chozos* of Andalucía. If you can get fresh shrimps, use the broth in which you cook them to make the sauce.

makes 20-25 croquettes / serves 4 as a starter

the filling
5 tablespoons olive oil
4 rounded tablespoons flour
2 tablespoons sherry or white wine
450 ml/¾ pint/2 cups fish broth
3-4 tablespoons peeled cooked shrimps, chopped if large
1 tablespoon chopped parsley
About 1 tablespoon pimentón
salt and pepper

the coating
4 rounded tablespoons seasoned flour
1 large egg
6 tablespoons toasted breadcrumbs
oil for frying

Heat the oil in a saucepan. Stir in the flour and let it froth up for a moment. Stir in the sherry or wine and bubble up. Gradually whisk in the rest of the liquid till smooth. Cook over a gentle heat, stirring with a wooden spoon, until you have a very thick, glossy sauce. Stir in the chopped shrimps, parsley and enough pimentón to turn the sauce pink. Season with salt and pepper.

Spread the mixture on a plate and cover with clingfilm. Leave to cool and firm in the fridge for an hour or two – overnight if possible.

When you are ready to cook, spread the flour on one plate, fork up the egg with its own volume of water on a second, and the breadcrumbs on a third.

With a knife, cut the filling into 20-25 short stubby fingers. Roll each finger first in the flour, and then in the egg mixture, and finally press it firmly into the breadcrumbs. Continue until the filling is all used up. Leave in a cool place for an hour or two to set the coating.

Heat enough oil to submerge the croquettes. When it is lightly hazed with blue, add the croquettes a few at a time – not too many or the oil temperature will drop. Fry them crisp and golden brown.

Serve the croquettes piping hot from the pan.

Chicken croquettes
Croquetas de pollo

Spanish boiling fowls are small and well-flavoured but tough. They are jointed and simmered with pulses and fresh vegetables and often served like the French *pot-au-feu*: first a bowl of strong broth, followed by the meat and vegetables as a second course. Leftovers from the Sunday boiled chicken – *puchero* – go to make *croquetas* for Monday. Make double quantities for the freezer.

makes 20-25 croquettes / serves 3-4 as a starter

the filling
5 tablespoons olive oil
4 rounded tablespoons flour
450 ml/¾ pint/2 cups chicken broth
about 4 tablespoons finely-chopped cooked chicken
1 teaspoon grated nutmeg
salt and pepper

the coating
3-4 tablespoons seasoned plain (all-purpose) flour
1 large egg forked with 2 tablespoons milk
4-5 tablespoons toasted breadcrumbs
oil for frying

Heat the oil or butter in a saucepan. Stir in the flour and let it froth up for a moment. Beat in the liquid gradually with a wooden spoon. Cook over a gentle heat until you have a very thick soft sauce – the more skilful you become, the thinner you can make the sauce, and the more delicate the croquettes will be.

Stir in the chopped chicken, parsley and nutmeg. Taste and add salt and pepper. Spread the mixture on a plate and cover it with another inverted plate. Leave to cool and firm in the fridge for an hour or two – overnight if possible.

When you are ready to cook, spread the seasoned flour on one plate, the egg-and-milk on a second, and the breadcrumbs on a third.

With a knife, mark the chicken sauce into 20-25 short stubby fingers. Roll each finger first in the flour, and then in the egg mixture, and finally press it firmly into the breadcrumbs. All surfaces should be well coated or the croquette will burst in the hot oil. Continue until the sauce is all used up. Leave in a cool place for an hour or two to set the coating.

Heat just enough olive oil in a frying pan (skillet) to submerge the croquettes. When the surface is lightly hazed with blue, slip in the croquettes a few at a time – not too many or the oil temperature will drop. Fry them crisp and golden brown.

Serve the croquettes piping hot from the pan.

Tuna croquettes
Croquetas de atún

This particular recipe comes from a small bar-restaurant outside La Linea. Its vine-covered terrace overlooks the Bay of Gibraltar, which perhaps explains the inclusion of that most British of seasonings, Worcestershire sauce. Make extra for freezing.

makes 20-25 croquettes / serves 4 as a starter

the filling
200 g/7 oz can of tuna in oil or brine
5 tablespoons olive oil
4 rounded tablespoons flour
450 ml/¾ pint/2 cups fish broth
few drops Worcestershire sauce
salt and pepper

the coating
4 tablespoons seasoned flour
1 large egg
4-5 tablespoons toasted breadcrumbs
oil for frying

Drain and flake the tuna and set it aside.

Heat the oil in a small saucepan. Stir in the flour and let it froth up for a moment. Beat in the liquid gradually with a wooden spoon. Cook over a gentle heat until you have a very thick soft sauce (the thinner you can make the sauce, the more delicate the croquettes will be).

Stir in the flaked tuna and season with Worcestershire sauce. Taste and add salt and pepper. Spread the mixture on a plate and cover with clingfilm. Leave to cool and firm in the fridge for an hour or two – overnight if possible.

When you are ready to cook, spread the flour on one plate, the egg forked up with its own volume of water on a second, and the breadcrumbs on a third.

With a knife mark the chicken sauce into 20-25 short stubby fingers. Roll each finger first in the flour, and then in the egg mixture, and finally press it firmly into the breadcrumbs. Continue until the sauce is all used up. Leave in a cool place for an hour or two to set the coating.

In a heavy frying pan (skillet), heat enough oil to submerge the croquettes. When it is lightly hazed with blue, slip in a few croquettes at a time. Fry them until crisp and golden. Continue till all are done and serve piping hot.

Cheese croquettes
Croquetas de queso

Spain has a large repertoire of matured hard cheeses of which the best-known is Manchego, a ewe's milk cheese from the central plateau of La Mancha. The little fine-flavoured pieces from near the rind go into this economical but delicious treat. Make a batch for the freezer – they de-frost in a moment.

makes 20-25 croquettes / serves 3-4 as a starter

the filling
5 tablespoons olive oil or melted butter
4 rounded tablespoons flour
4 tablespoons dry sherry or white wine
300 ml/½ pint/1 cup chicken broth or milk
3-4 tablespoons grated cheese (Manchego for preference)
1 tablespoon grated onion (optional)
salt and pepper

the coating
3-4 tablespoons seasoned flour
1 egg, beaten with 2 tablespoons milk
4-5 tablespoons toasted breadcrumbs
oil for frying

to serve
fresh tomato sauce (page 176)

Heat the oil or butter in a saucepan. Stir in the flour and let it froth up for a moment. Beat in the sherry or wine and bubble up. Add the rest of the liquid gradually with a wooden spoon. Stir in the grated cheese and onion (if used). Cook over a gentle heat until you have a very thick soft sauce. Taste and add salt and pepper.

Spread the mixture on a plate and cover with clingfilm. Leave to cool and firm in the fridge for an hour or two – overnight if possible.

When you are ready to cook, spread the flour on one plate, the egg forked up with its own volume of milk or water on a second, and the breadcrumbs on a third.

With a knife, mark the filling into 20-25 short stubby fingers. Roll each finger first in the flour, and then in the egg mixture, and finally press it firmly into the breadcrumbs. Make sure each croquette is thoroughly coated. Continue until the filling is all used up.

In a frying pan or skillet, heat enough oil to just submerge the croquettes. When the surface is lightly hazed with blue, add the croquettes a few at a time – not too many or the oil temperature will drop. Fry them crisp and golden and serve them straight from the pan.

Ham croquettes
Croquetas de jamón

These are usually made with the well-flavoured scrag ends of the salt-cured mountain ham, jamón serrano, which is the most valuable flavouring ingredient in the Spanish kitchen. The liquor for the basic sauce is often the broth made with a ham bone – nothing is wasted in the Spanish kitchen. Make extra for freezing.

Makes 20-25 croquettes / serves 3-4 as a starter

the filling
5 tablespoons olive oil or pork-dripping
4 rounded tablespoons flour
2-3 tablespoons finely chopped serrano ham

450 ml/¾ pint/2 cups ham or chicken broth
1 hard-boiled egg, chopped finely (optional)
salt and pepper
the coating
3-4 tablespoons seasoned plain (all-purpose) flour
1 egg, beaten with 2 tablespoons milk
4-5 tablespoons toasted breadcrumbs
oil for frying

Heat the oil or dripping in a small heavy saucepan. Stir in the flour and let it fry for a moment without taking colour. Beat in the broth gradually with a wooden spoon and stir in the ham. Cook over a gentle heat until you have a very thick soft sauce.

Stir in the chopped egg, if used. Taste and add salt and pepper. Spread the mixture on a plate and cover with clingfilm. Leave to cool and firm in the fridge for an hour or two – overnight if possible.

When you are ready to cook, spread the flour on one plate, the egg-and-milk on a second, and the breadcrumbs on a third.

With a knife, mark the filling into 20-25 short stubby fingers. Roll each finger first in the flour, and then in the egg mixture, and finally press it firmly into the breadcrumbs. Check that all surfaces are well coated. Continue until the sauce is all used up. Set in a cool place for an hour or two to firm the coating.

In a frying pan (skillet), heat enough oil to just submerge the croquettes. When it is lightly hazed with blue, slip in a few of the croquettes – not too many at once or the oil temperature will drop and the croquettes will burst. Fry them until crisp.

Serve the croquettes hot from the pan.

Mushroom croquettes
Croquetas de setas

I have had these made with porcini mushrooms in Barcelona, saffron milkcaps in Valencia and field mushrooms in Andalucía, but the best were those perfumed with freshly-grated truffle served in a small bar set into the wall of the fortified town of Morella in the mountains of the Levante region. At the time, some thirty years ago, the inhabitants of the town didn't much rate their precious crop since, though the fungi was available in considerable quantity under the scrub oak in the cistus scrub, it had been used as meat-substitute in the bean-pot during the bad days of the Civil War.

makes 20-25 croquettes / serves 3-4 as a starter

the filling
5 tablespoons olive oil or 150 g/5 oz/½ cup butter
generous handful of mushrooms (wild or cultivated), diced
4 rounded tablespoons flour
1 wine glass of dry sherry
300 ml/½ pint/1 cup chicken or ham broth
2 tablespoons chopped parsley
salt and pepper
the coating
3-4 tablespoons seasoned flour
1 large egg
4-5 tablespoons toasted breadcrumbs
oil for frying

Heat the oil or butter in a saucepan. Sauté the mushrooms briefly. Stir in the flour and fry it for a moment. Add the sherry and beat in the rest of the liquid gradually with a wooden spoon. Cook over a gentle heat until you have a very thick smooth sauce. Stir in the parsley. Check the seasoning and add salt and pepper.

Spread the mixture on a plate and cover with clingfilm. Leave to cool and firm in the fridge for an hour or two – overnight if possible.

When you are ready to cook, spread the flour on one plate, the egg forked up with its own volume of milk or water on a second, and the breadcrumbs on a third.

With a knife, mark the mushroom mixture into 20-25 short stubby fingers. Roll each finger first in the flour, and then in the egg mixture, and finally press it firmly into the breadcrumbs. Make sure all surfaces are well coated.

Continue until the filling is all used up. Leave aside in a cool place for an hour or two to set the coating.

In a frying pan or skillet, heat enough oil to just submerge the croquettes. When the oil is lightly hazed with blue, slip in the croquettes a few at a time or the oil temperature will drop. Fry them until golden brown.

Serve the croquettes as soon as they come out of the pan.

Spiced meat pasties
Empanadillas de Orense

The spicy meat filling for these pasties is typically Gallician. To wrap it, I give one of the simplest of Spanish pastry doughs. Sometimes these doughs are raised with yeast, like a bread dough, but this warm-water crust is more like those used for English pork pies. The recipe can be adapted to make one large rectangular pie for cutting into squares: if so it will need longer baking at a slightly lower temperature – follow the instructions on page 200.

makes 25-30 bite-sized pasties / serves 5-6 as a starter

the filling
2 tablespoons olive oil
1 medium onion, diced
1 garlic clove, crushed and chopped
1 large or 2 smallish red peppers, de-seeded and diced
2 tablespoons diced serrano ham or lean bacon
1 link soft chorizo or similar, skinned and mashed
250 g/8 oz lean pork or veal or lamb, cubed small
1 wine glass of white wine or dry cider
a dozen saffron threads, soaked in 1 tablespoon boiling water
1 teaspoon thyme
salt and pepper

the oil pastry
300 g/10 oz/2½ cups self-raising flour, plus extra for rolling
1 level teaspoon salt
4 tablespoons olive oil, plus extra for greasing
2 tablespoons white wine
150 ml/¼ pint/⅔ cup milk or water

First make the filling. Heat the oil in a frying pan (skillet) and gently fry the onion, garlic and peppers. When the vegetables are soft, push them to one side and add the ham or bacon and chorizo and continue to fry till the fat melts. Add the meat and fry till it firms and takes a little colour. Splash in the wine or sherry, and add the saffron with its water. Bubble up, add the thyme, season with salt and pepper, turn down the heat, lid loosely and simmer until the liquid has almost all evaporated and the meat is tender. Leave aside to cool.

Preheat the oven to Gas Mark 6/200°C/400°F.

Now make the pastry: make a well in the flour and mix in the salt. Put the oil, wine and milk or water into a small pan and heat to blood temperature. Pour the warm liquid into the well in the flour and work the dry and wet ingredients together until you have a soft elastic dough. While it's still warm, roll the pastry out thinly on a well-floured board with a rolling pin (or roll between 2 sheets of clingfilm). Cut the pastry into rounds about the size of a coffee-saucer with a pastry cutter or sharp-edged wine glass. Place a teaspoon of the filling into the centre of each round. Wet the edges and fold one half over the other to enclose the filling. Mark the edges with a fork to seal. Transfer the pasties to an oiled baking sheet, brush the tops (if you like) with a little egg-and-milk and prick the tops with a fork.

Bake in the oven for 10-15 minutes, until the pastry is golden brown. Or you can, if you prefer, deep-fry the pasties as you would croquettes.

Spiced mincemeat pasties
Empanadillas de picadillo

These were one of my favourite snacks when I was a schoolgirl and my family lived in Madrid. My stepfather was attached to the Embassy and my mother's cook used to make them for the endless cocktail parties which were part of the diplomats' social round.

makes 25-30 bite-sized pasties / serves 5-6 as a starter
2 tablespoons olive oil, plus extra for greasing
1 garlic clove, chopped
1 small onion, chopped finely
250 g/8 oz finely-chopped pork
1 level tablespoon flour
1 tablespoon raisins, soaked to swell
1 small glass sherry
1 tablespoon toasted pine kernels or flaked almonds
1 teaspoon ground cinnamon
½ teaspoon ground cloves
About 500 g/1 lb ready-made pastry
salt and pepper

Heat the oil in a small frying pan or skillet. Fry the garlic and onion for a few moments; then add the meat. Turn it until it changes colour and the moisture evaporates. Stir in the flour and fry it till it froths. Add the raisins and the sherry, bubble up to evaporate the alcohol and thicken the juices. Stir in the nuts and the spices. Season with salt and pepper and bubble up to blend the flavours, add a glass of water, bubble up again, lid loosely and cook gently for 15-20 minutes to tenderise the meat. Leave aside to cool.

Preheat the oven to Gas Mark 6/200°C/400°F.

Roll out the pastry thinly on a well-floured board or between 2 sheets of clingfilm, and cut it into small rounds with a sharp-edged wine glass. Drop teaspoons of the stuffing onto one side of each round. Dampen the edges of the pastry and fold one half over the other to enclose the filling. Press the edges together with a fork.

Arrange the pasties on a well-greased baking sheet. Bake in the oven for 10-15 minutes, until the pastry is well gilded.

Note: if you prefer, fry the pasties in shallow oil, turning them once.

Tuna and tomato pasties
Empanadillas de Valencia

Little pasties stuffed with conserved tuna in a rich tomato sauce are a speciality of the ports of the Levante region, of which Valencia is the capital. The inshore fleet of the Mediterranean landed vast quantities of the beautiful silver-flanked tuna which, until recent years, migrated in huge shoals from the Atlantic through the Pillars of Hercules on the way to their spawning grounds in the Black Sea. The catch was originally barreled up with salt for storage, or (later) canned under oil, and remains a store cupboard staple of the Mediterranean kitchen.

makes 25-30 bite-sized pasties / serves 5-6 as a starter
Approx. 200 g/7 oz can of tuna
1 tablespoon olive oil, plus extra for greasing
1 garlic clove, chopped finely
1 tablespoon chopped onion
500 g/1 lb tomatoes, skinned and chopped (fresh or canned)
1 teaspoon thyme
1 teaspoon chopped parsley
500 g/1 lb ready-made pastry
flour for dusting
salt and pepper

Make the filling first. Drain the tuna, flake with a fork, and reserve.

Heat the oil in a frying pan or skillet, add the garlic and onion and fry gently till the vegetables take a little colour. Add the tomatoes and thyme and bubble up over a high heat, mashing with a wooden spoon till the tomatoes melt into a thick rich sauce. Stir in the tuna flakes and parsley. Taste and season. Leave aside to cool.

Preheat the oven to Gas Mark 6/200°C/400°F.

Roll out the pastry thinly on a well-floured board, and cut it into small rounds with a sharp-edged wine glass. Drop teaspoons of the filling onto one side of each round. Dampen the edges and fold one half over the other to enclose the filling. Press the edges together with a fork.

Arrange the pasties on a well-greased baking sheet and prick the tops with a fork (brush with a little egg and milk if you like a pretty glaze). Bake in the oven for 10-15 minutes, until the pastry is crisp and brown.

Gallician pork pie
Empanada de lomo

This is Galicia's most traditional pie, still popular today, though most people buy theirs from the baker, where big trays of it appear at midday. You can make it in the form of individual pasties (*empanadillas*), following the instructions on page 196, or, as here, as a rectangular pie (*empanada*) for cutting. Either way it's lovely picnic food, as well as a delicious tapa.

makes 18–20 tapa portions / serves 4 as a starter
500 g/1 lb lean pork, cubed small
2 wine glasses of white wine
½ teaspoon thyme
1 teaspoon chopped marjoram
1 tablespoon hot pimentón or chilli powder
3 tablespoons olive oil
1 medium onion, slivered
1 garlic clove, chopped
1 green pepper, de-seeded and diced

½ teaspoon salt
1 large potato, peeled and diced
500 g/1 lb ready-made pastry
flour for rolling

Put the pork to marinate overnight in the wine, herbs and pimentón and a tablespoon of the olive oil.

Drain the meat, reserving the marinade.

Fry the onion, garlic and green pepper in the rest of the olive oil until they take a little colour. Push the vegetables to one side. Add the meat and turn it in the hot oil until it begins to fry. Sprinkle in the salt. Pour in the marinade, bubble up, turn down the heat, and cover. Leave to simmer for 20-25 minutes until the meat is tender. Add the potato cubes and simmer until the potato is tender. Remove the lid and bubble up until the juices have nearly all evaporated. Taste and adjust the seasoning. Leave aside to cool.

Preheat the oven to Gas Mark 5/190°C/375°F.

Divide the pastry in half and roll out each piece on a well-floured board into two rectangles, one a little smaller than the other to fit a 25 cm/10 inch square non-stick baking tin or equivalent rectangle and line it with the larger piece of pastry. Spread on the filling, leaving a margin all round. Dampen the margin and lay the second sheet on top. Press the edges together, dampen the edge and fold it over again to make a thick rim. Pinch the rim at intervals to make a scalloped edge. Prick the top with a fork. Brush, if you like a pretty glaze, with a little egg forked up with milk.

Bake in the oven for 25-30 minutes, until the pastry is crisp and well gilded. Serve hot or cold, cut into squares.

Spinach pasties
Empanadillas de espinacas

Pasties can be made with a wide variety of pre-cooked vegetables: chard stalks and leaves, sliced leeks with shredded cabbage, puréed aubergine (eggplant) or mashed potatoes mixed with onion and parsley. Fillings may or may not include cheese for protein and egg to bind.

makes 25-30 bite-sized pasties / serves 6 as a starter

4 large handfuls spinach leaves
2 tablespoons olive oil
1 garlic clove, crushed
2 tablespoons dry sherry
½ teaspoon grated nutmeg
juice of 1 lemon
2 tablespoons grated cheese (manchego for preference)
1 large egg, forked to blend
500 g/1lb pastry (short, puff, bread dough, or Spanish
on page 196)
flour for rolling
salt and pepper

Preheat the oven to Gas Mark 6/200°C/400°F.

Rinse the spinach leaves, pinch off any thick stalks, and pack them into a roomy pan with the oil, garlic, sherry, nutmeg and lemon juice. Add a little salt, lid tightly and shake the pan over the heat till the leaves wilt. Remove the lid and bubble up to evaporate excess moisture. Leave to cool, then chop roughly and mix in the cheese and egg.

Meanwhile, roll out the pastry thinly on a well-floured board, and cut into small rounds with a sharp-edged wine glass. Drop teaspoonfuls of the spinach mixture onto one side of each round. Dampen the edges of the pastry and fold one half over the other to enclose the filling. Press the edges together with a fork and prick the tops.

Arrange the pasties on a non-stick baking sheet (you can glaze the tops with a little egg and milk if you like). Bake in the oven for 10-15 minutes, until the pastry is well gilded.

Note: if you prefer, fry the pasties in shallow oil, turning them once.

Cheese fritters
Buñuelos de queso

These crisp little morsels, simply made and quickly prepared, must be enjoyed hot from the fryer.

makes 15-20 fritters / serves 3-4 as a starter

3 large eggs
3 tablespoons milk
6 tablespoons grated cheese
(manchego for preference)
3 tablespoons flour
1 tablespoon chopped parsley
1 tablespoon grated onion
1 tablespoon pimentón (mild or hot)
oil for frying
salt and pepper

Fork the eggs and milk together till well-blended. Stir in the cheese. Work in the flour, whisking to avoid lumps. Add the parsley, onion and pimentón. Season with salt and pepper.

Heat enough oil in a roomy pan to float the fritters. When it is lightly hazed with blue, drop in teaspoons of the mixture – just so many as will float on the surface. Remove to kitchen paper with a draining spoon as soon they puff up and brown.

Ham and cheese fritters
Delicias de jamón y queso

A dish for those in a hurry, this is a combination of *pain perdu* and *croque monsieur* – lovely and crisp and delicious.

makes 8 small sandwiches /
serves 2 as a light summer meal

8 slices bread
about 4 slices serrano ham
about 4 slivers mature manchego cheese
1 large egg
2 tablespoons milk
4-5 tablespoons olive oil
salt and pepper

Make sandwiches with the bread, ham and cheese, and cut them neatly into quarters. Beat the egg with the milk and season it with salt and pepper.

Dip the sandwiches in the egg mixture. Fry them in the oil, turning once, until golden brown on both sides.

Serve piping hot, spiked with cocktail sticks.

Frittered prawns
Gambas en gabadina

This recipe makes the most of luxuriously expensive deep-water prawns. If you manage to find raw ones, use the cooking water to replace the plain water.

makes 12 tapa portions / serves 3-4 as a starter

12 large prawns, cooked but unshelled
1 small glass of dry sherry

1 bay leaf
1-2 celery stalks, chopped
½ medium onion, chunked
½ teaspoon peppercorns
4 tablespoons olive oil
3 tablespoons flour
milk
salt

the coating
3-4 tablespoons seasoned flour
1 large egg
4-5 tablespoons toasted breadcrumbs
oil for frying

to serve
quartered lemons

Shell the prawns, leaving the tails in place. Put the debris (including the heads) in a small pan with the sherry, a couple of tumblers of water, bay, celery, onion and peppercorns. Add a little salt. Bring to the boil, turn the heat down and simmer, loosely covered, for 15-20 minutes to make a little stock. Strain out the solids, pressing down to extract all the juice. Return the broth to the pan and bubble up until you have 2-3 tablespoons of well-flavoured fish stock. Add enough milk to make it up to 450 ml (2 cups) of liquid, the basis for the coating sauce.

To prepare the coating sauce, heat the olive oil in a small pan. Stir in the flour and let it froth up for a moment. Whisk in the warm stock-and-milk gradually till smooth and lump-free. Cook over a gentle heat, stirring with a wooden spoon, until thick enough to coat the spoon. Leave to cool to finger heat.

Dip the prawns in the sauce, coating them all over but leaving the tails exposed. Set them to cool and firm in the freezer or coldest part of the fridge for an hour or two.

Spread the flour on one plate; fork up the egg with its own volume of milk on a second, and spread the breadcrumbs on a third.

Dust each coated prawn first through the flour, and then in the egg mixture, and then press it firmly into the breadcrumbs.

In a frying pan or skillet, heat enough oil to just submerge the jacketed prawns. When the surface is lightly hazed with blue, slip in the prawns a few at a time. Fry at a medium heat until the coating is crisp and brown. Transfer to kitchen paper to drain and serve the prawns hot from the pan, with quartered lemons.

Salt cod fritters
Buñuelos de bacalao

Salt cod, known as 'mountain fish', *pez de monte*, for its keeping qualities far from the sea, was the fasting food of the Catholic shores of the Mediterranean throughout the Middle Ages, a trade of great economic importance. The recipes were so good that the taste for them remains. Fresh cod can substitute for salted if the latter is hard to find (it can be rather expensive). To soak your own, allow 48 hours in several changes of fresh cold water.

makes 20-24 fritters / serves 4-5 as a starter
1 kg/2 lb floury potatoes, peeled and chunked
500 g/1 lb ready-soaked middle-cut salt cod (bacalao)
2 medium eggs, forked to blend
4 rounded tablespoons self-raising flour
1 garlic clove, crushed
1 tablespoon grated onion
1 tablespoon chopped parsley
½ teaspoon grated nutmeg
oil for frying
salt and pepper
chilli sauce, to serve

Put the chunked potatoes in a roomy pan with enough water to cover. Bring to the boil and place the piece of bacalao on the top.

Lid and cook till the potatoes are tender and the fish has softened. Remove the fish and reserve, and drain the potatoes. Bone, skin and flake the fish and mash it into the potatoes. Allow to cool to finger heat, then work in the eggs and flour, beating till smooth. Beat in the garlic, onion, parsley and nutmeg and a little pepper. Taste and add salt if necessary.

In a frying pan or skillet, heat enough oil to float the fritters. When it is lightly hazed with blue, drop in teaspoons of the fritter mixture. Turn them when they are puffed up and crisp. Drain on kitchen paper. Serve piping hot, with chilli sauce handed separately.

CHOOSING YOUR TAPAS

Back in Britain in the early 1980's, my family and I continued to enjoy the Spanish way with tapas, adapting them to our needs in a city, London, which at the time, had not yet discovered the pleasures of such an informal way of eating. One of the chief recommendations of tapas to the home-cook is adaptablity. There's virtually nothing which tastes good and is savoury rather than sweet which cannot be presented in tapa form. There are many dishes which require a minimum of preparation and cooking, or can be prepared ahead, and some which freeze well – and, since the portions are always small and individual, they can be unfrozen fast. Tapas are perfect for parties – a trouble-free way of providing for an expandable number of guests. Or simply to add entertainment to an ordinary meal shared with a friend. A dish or two of something which needs no cooking – marinated olives, a slice of cured ham or sausage, a bit of potato salad – staves off the pangs of hunger until you have prepared something hot and delicious. And if more people arrive meanwhile, well, more bread and another small dish can be put out, and maybe a tortilla or a plate of hot French fries added to the menu. When it's all on the table, the cook can sit down and pick and share with the guests.

When serving tapas as a party meal, a fair rule of thumb is to make as many main dishes as you have guests. Either set out most of the dishes at the same time, buffet-style, bringing in a hot one or two later. Or organise the meal into the familiar two courses, starting with the little basic tapas of olives, nuts, cheese and ham, plus salads and cold dishes. By the time you bring in the main dishes, your guests will have accustomed themselves to this delightful informal eating, and will happily organise their own platefuls. Provide plenty of good bread for people to mop up sauces and wipe fingers.

While a chilled glass of dry manzanilla or sherry – fino, oloroso – is the natural partner to a tapa in its land of origin, a good Spanish red or white wine or even cider or beer are also perfectly acceptable. Spaniards also set water and extra glasses on the table when drinking wine – all the wine-producing nations take wine and water alternately, a sensible precaution reinforced by the soothing effect of olive oil on the digestive system when used, as is usual throughout the Mediterranean, for enrichment as well as a cooking medium.

Winter tapa party

Here's some lovely warming spicy food, mostly from the high central plateau of Spain, where the winters are cold. The oxtail stew is delicious on a winter night. It can be prepared well ahead, as can everything but the shrimp fritters.

serves 6-8
Olives (page 12)
Spiced peanuts (page 15)
Cabrales or any blue cheese from the Picos (page 18)
Rice salad with tuna (page 54)
Black pudding (page 26)
Baked potatoes with oil and onion (page 64)
Gratin of cardoons or chard (page 76)
Spiced oxtail stew (page 162)
Gallician pork pie (page 199)
Meatballs in tomato sauce (page 144)
Shrimp fritters (page 136)

Spring tapa party

Spring offers a lovely opportunity to serve young vegetables. Look for scarlet radishes, baby courgettes (zucchini) and carrots, early asparagus and peppers, and young broad and green beans, to serve raw. Wash the vegetables carefully, and present them complete with any leaves flanked by a dish of coarse salt, quartered lemons and a flagon of first-pressing virgin olive oil so that guests can dip or dress their own as they please.

serves 6-8

Olives (page 12)
Raw baby vegetables with lemon, olive oil and sea salt
Mahon cheese or manchego under oil (page 18)
Cod's roe salad (page 43)
Spinach or chard leaves dressed with vinegar (page 82)
New potatoes with garlic and saffron (page 77)
Crayfish with green sauce (page 135)
Fisherman's mussels (page 132)
Grilled (broiled) spiced hamburgers (page 145)
Griddled marinated lamb's kidneys (page 158)

Summer tapa party

As with the spring tapa party, look for fresh young vegetables to serve raw with good oil, lemon quarters and coarse salt. Chicken or rabbit with garlic is my favourite summer dish – for a delicious al fresco lunch, take the raw ingredients outside and cook it on the barbecue or a little fire.

serves 6-8

Olives (page 12)
Crisp salad leaves with lemon, olive oil and sea salt
Casero cheese (matured goat's cheese)
Fried baby artichokes (page 72)

Russian salad with mayonnaise (page 38)
Green beans with spiced almonds (page 83)
Chicken with garlic (page 170)
Clams in sherry (page 128)
Steaks with blue cheese (page 146)
Grilled (broiled) prawns (page 124)
Moorish kebabs (page 159)

Autumn tapa party

Almonds and smoked cheese, mushrooms and quail spell the pleasures of autumn. In September the grapes are harvested round Jerez, ready for the labour of love which converts the raw juice into the clear dry aromatic wines which go so well with these dishes.

serves 6-8
Olives (page 12)
Salted almonds (page 16)
Smoked Idiazábal or other smoked cheese (page 18)
Griddled soft chorizo or sausages (page 25)
Rice salad with pine kernels (page 51)
Whole broad bean casserole (page 90)
Basque crab (page 138)
Spiced mincemeat pasties (page 195)
Mushroom croquettes (page 192)
Deep-fried spatchcocked quails (page 172)
Grilled (broiled) lamb cutlets with garlic mayonnaise
(page 149)

A children's tapa party

Children are the most demanding audience a cook ever has to face. They will often eat only those things which are familiar to them, and are deeply conservative when confronted with the new. To counteract such prejudices, I always make plenty of big fat French fries, for which most children have an insatiable appetite. Otherwise, all these recipes are easily recognisable for what they are.

serves 6-8

Toasted hazelnuts (page 18)
Fresh white cheese (page 18)
Potato crisps (page 29)
Pork scratchings (page 28)
Cherry tomatoes mimosa (page 42)
Fried quail's eggs (page 109)
Ham and cheese fritters (page 204)
Breadcrumbed chicken (page 171)
French fries (page 78)
Fresh sausages (page 28)

Vegetarian tapa party

Spain likes its fish and meat, and rarely has a meal which does not include one or the other, even if it's only a chunk of ham bone for flavouring. Careful selection, however, can produce a delicious vegetarian meal – there are also plenty of recipes which can be turned vegetarian by judiciously omitting the ham or bacon which flavours them.

serves 6-8

Olives (page 12)
Hot bread with olive oil and garlic (page 30)
New potato salad (page 50)
Artichokes in oil (page 50)
Mixed vegetable omelette (page 108)
Spinach pasties (page 200)
Cheese fritters (page 202)
Courgettes (zucchini) in tomato sauce (page 86)
Aubergine (eggplant) purée (page 68)
Baked mushrooms with parsley and garlic (page 65)

Slimmers' tapas

Spanish cooks are increasingly health-conscious, but do not naturally regard good food with a view to its potential for slimmers. Here is a meal which avoids the obvious high-calorie foods and uses the grill rather than the frying pan or skillet.

serves 4

Olives (page 12)
Winkles with spiced vinegar (page 130)
Salad skewers (page 56)
Tomatoes with garlic and marjoram (page 58)
Seafood salad (page 60)
Monkfish kebabs (page 118)
Grilled (broiled) prawns and shellfish (page 124)
Spiced grilled (broiled) chicken (page 168)

No-cook tapas

An excellent tapa-selection can be produced just by opening a few cans and slicing a tomato or two. Make sure all ingredients are the best quality you can afford. The simpler the recipe, the more important the basic materials.

serves 4

Olives (page 12)
Serrano or pata negra ham (page 21)
Chorizo (page 24)
Roncal or Manchego cheese (page 18)
Beetroot salad (page 52)
Tomatoes with anchovies (page 57)
Canned sardines with onion (page 34)
Canapés of conserved tuna (page 32)
Roast pork and crisps (page 158)

Tapas for two

Two-person tapas is a good opportunity to experiment with recipes requiring luxury ingredients which you wouldn't want to risk in larger quantities.

Olives (page 12)
Cabrales with chicory (page 54)
Asparagus with soft-boiled eggs (page 71)
Tomatoes with anchovies (page 57)
Peppery potatoes (page 80)
Oysters under breadcrumbs and garlic (page 126)
Prawns in oil and chilli (page 134)
Grilled (broiled) lamb cutlets with garlic mayonnaise
(page 149)

Tapas for eight or more

When you are dealing with a crowd of people, increase the amounts of two or three of the dishes, rather than adding yet another one to the list. Here I suggest three deep-fried dishes – squid, shrimp and aubergine fritters – since once you have the oil hot, it's easy enough to carry on frying. Any other dishes best eaten warm can be kept in a low oven until you are ready.

Olives (page 12)
Jamón serrano or chorizo (page 21)
Spiced peanuts (page 15)
Meatballs in tomato sauce (page 144)
Potato mayonnaise with red peppers (page 39)
Tortilla(s) of your choice (pages 94-108)
Fried calamar (page 126)
Shrimp fritters (page 136)
Aubergine (eggplant) fritters (page 68)

Spiced meat pasties (page 194)
Chicken with red peppers (page 169)
Veal kidneys with sherry (page 156)

Tapas for four

Four is a good number for a tapa party – it gives the opportunity for a little choice without putting too great a strain on the budget. The salads and vegetable dishes are easily prepared ahead of time, and the croquettes can also be made ahead ready to be deep-fried at the last minute, while you keep an eye on the fish steaks and pork medallions as they cook.

Olives (page 12)
Salted almonds (page 16)
Tomatoes with anchovies (page 57)
Eggs with mayonnaise (page 40)
Broad beans with ham (page 74)
Fried green peppers or baby artichokes
(page 66 and 72)
Chicken croquettes (page 187)
Griddled tuna or swordfish steaks (page 112)
Pork medallions with lemon and marjoram (page 152)

Tapas for six

All these recipes can be prepared ahead of time. The tortilla, peppers and tomatoes are best served at room temperature, the prawns need no more than heating in their oil, while the kebabs and marinated porkfillet need nothing more than finishing in or under a high heat and are transferred direct from stove to table.

Olives (page 12)
Manchego or matured Casero cheese (page 18)

Salted almonds (page 16)
Beetroot salad (page 52)
Fresh-pickled anchovies (page 44)
Potato tortilla (page 94)
Fried peppers (page 66)
Tomatoes stuffed with pine kernels (page 84)
Prawns in oil and chilli (page 134)
Chicken kebabs (page 176)
Marinated griddled pork fillet (page 154)

INDEX